DADVENTURES

Amazing outdoor adventures for daring dads and fearless kids

ALEX GREGORY

HarperCollins*Publishers*

HarperCollins*Publishers*
1 London Bridge Street
London SE1 9GF

www.harpercollins.co.uk

First published by HarperCollins*Publishers* 2018

13 5 7 9 10 8 6 4 2

A catalogue record of this book is
available from the British Library

HB ISBN 978-0-00-828370-4
EB ISBN 978-0-00-828371-1

Printed and bound in Great Britain by
CPI Group (UK) Ltd, Croydon

MIX
Paper from
responsible sources
FSC
www.fsc.org
FSC C007454

This book is produced from independently certified FSC paper
to ensure responsible forest management.

For more information visit: www.harpercollins.co.uk/green

To my parents and grandparents, who showed me the value of being outdoors.

For my children, Jasper, Daisy and Jesse. Here's to making many more happy memories together under the big blue sky.

ABOUT THE AUTHOR

Alex Gregory MBE is a two-time Olympic gold medallist, five-time World champion and World record holder for the Great Britain Men's rowing team. In August 2017 he took part in The Polar Row, a pioneering Arctic rowing expedition in which he and his crew successfully forged a route across previously un-rowed Arctic waters, including the northern-most recorded point ever reached by a rowing vessel, breaking numerous world records in the process. Alex has now retired from competitive sport and is focusing his attentions on inspiring others to achieve their full potential and expressing his insights through motivational speaking. His three children, Jasper, Daisy and Jesse, have been a huge motivation for him pursuing another passion of his, living and experiencing the outdoors. As a Fellow of the British Exploring Society (a charity aiming to provide young people with an intense and lasting experience of self-discovery in wilderness environments) Alex is intent on sharing his knowledge, experience and enthusiasm for the outdoors and the fantastic benefits that time outdoors brings to the whole family.

CONTENTS

NOTE

In descriptions of the activities in this book I've generally assumed that you have one child of a particular age. You might, of course, have a number of children of a varying range of ages. Each activity can easily be tailored to fit the needs of multiple children of any age.

KEY TO ICONS

 Best in dry conditions

 Can be done in bad weather

 Best during the day

 Can be done at night

 Simple, no preparation needed

 For the more adventurous

 Can be done in the garden/close to home

 Involves wildlife

 Gadgets required

 Involves water

INTRODUCTION

*'You can't keep a toad under your bed,
it wouldn't be happy! Toads like
living in the garden!'*

A toad, by Jasper.

These could so easily have been my mum's words echoing around
our house as a seven-year-old me tried to smuggle a creature into my
room. But in reality this was a snatch of conversation I heard in the
upstairs of our home as my partner Emily tried to persuade our son
Jasper to put the toad he'd brought into his bedroom, back outside
into the front garden. Frogs and toads seem to be plentiful in the
small garden of our rented cottage, and they've provided us with
some exciting evening adventures. A few years ago, in our last house,
it was hedgehogs – and before that, well, there's always something to
do outdoors …

There are five of us in the house – two adults and three children – but a whole host of other creatures seem to have joined our menagerie along the way. Emily is the one who keeps us all going. She feeds us all, looks after us and stops our lives from grinding to a screeching halt.

We first met at university many years ago. As I was going into our housing block from early rowing-training sessions on the river, she'd be returning home from a night out with friends, living a far more typical university lifestyle than me. We'd stop and chat, and soon discovered that we got on very well. We enjoyed each other's company, and I found I wanted to spend more time with her than in a boat on the river. That was something new … and something that I couldn't ignore. We happily started to spend the rare free time we had together getting to know each other, understanding each other, and sharing dreams and future aspirations. Emily was incredibly patient. I was pursuing a seemingly impossible dream, meaning my free time was limited to almost nothing. This meant that very quickly in our relationship we recognised the value of quality time. My days were spent out on rivers, lakes or in the gym, essentially working a full-time job while at university. I didn't drink, I didn't socialise that much, I made as many lectures as I possibly could, but my life was focused on one specific thing: the Olympics.

I tried and I failed. Year after year I spent seven days a week, three times a day training, only to fall at the last hurdle. For so many different reasons I wasn't reaching my potential and was coming up well short of my goals. But I never gave up. When everyone disappeared off home for the university holidays, I remained, the only person in the block. Waking up that first morning was like a scene from a disaster movie in which everyone except me had disappeared. Emily had returned home to her family on the Isle of Wight, but I could never go back to my family home or go and visit hers because of training or racing. Thankfully, for me, Emily was prepared to stick with me as I pursued my sporting career on lakes and rivers in far-flung places around the world.

As time went by, we both graduated. Emily followed a career in teaching while I continued to battle it out for Olympic selection. We rented a tiny cottage in the centre of Henley-on-Thames and settled down, moving forward with our lives. Emily became an excellent primary-school teacher in a tough school on the outskirts of Reading, but things weren't going so well for me and my sporting career was on the ropes. In a world in which performance is everything I was certainly falling short, so it was with a great deal of luck that I was selected to travel with the 2008 Olympic rowing team to Beijing as reserve.

It seemed to be a bittersweet ending to my career, because after this trip I had decided to walk away from the sport for ever, as I was obviously not cut out for life as a successful Olympic rower. But it was there, sitting on the sidelines in China, that everything changed for me as an athlete – and for us as a couple. I returned home from China with renewed motivation and vigour, and set myself new goals, new challenges. I wasn't giving up just yet.

We weren't quite expecting what life had in store for us, as a few brief months after my trip as Olympic reserve we discovered we were going to have our first child.

It was a shock – a big shock – and not exactly in my grand plan. I had just found myself on a new path, and for the first time I was starting to excel in the sport I'd so nearly given up. There was a great deal of pressure on me to perform and I was only just beginning to do that, moving up the ranks within the team and reaching the position I'd need to be in to start competing for medals on the world stage. Life had taken an unexpected turn, and although I felt incredibly unsure about what it might entail, Emily remained strong and positive, matter of fact and excited about the future.

It was always going to happen at some point. We had talked about having children and starting family life together, but I never imagined it would be this soon and at our age. I was really worried about other people's reaction to our news, particularly my coach, Jürgen Gröbler, who demanded complete commitment and the very top level of performance on a consistent, daily basis. Would he think I was being unprofessional and not committed to my sport? My place in the GB rowing team felt under threat.

It took me six months to summon up the nerve to tell him, during which time I had further cemented my position as a valuable member of the squad and things had been going very well. I anxiously sat down and told him our news, shaking at the prospect of saying goodbye to nine years of commitment to rowing. To my utter surprise, astonishment and relief, Jürgen was happy and excited – even joyful – for us.

'Oh, Alex, zat is fantastic news,' he said in his strong German accent, eyes shining with genuine delight. 'I am so happy for you as a young family.'

The weight of the world was lifted off my shoulders. Jürgen had no idea what that meeting was like for me and how much his support at that moment meant. A month after I became world champion for the first time, our first child was born.

It was during Jasper's birth that I had to miss a day of training. I remember feeling terribly uncomfortable with this, despite having a fairly sound excuse. Emily was having a traumatic labour and the birth was far from easy. Seventy-two hours, a breakneck journey in an ambulance at 2 a.m., a whole load of screaming (mainly from me) and two hospitals later, Jasper was pulled out through emergency C-section.

Having been on a rollercoaster of emotion and not slept for days, I left my little family in the hospital and rocked up at the lake early in the morning acting as though everything was OK. I was an emotional wreck, relieved, happy, so tired but pumped full of adrenalin. My overriding wish, however, was to show that whatever was going on at home wasn't affecting my performance on the water or in the gym. I was back into training as normal, falling asleep behind the oar but exerting myself like my life depended on it. Your place in the British rowing team is never secure, so I didn't want to lose the position I was in after all those years of struggle. I spent the next eight months sleeping on our six-foot-long sofa (I'm six foot six) to try to limit the broken sleep while Emily dealt with the baby upstairs.

Daisy Delilah, our second child, came into the world four years later in 2013, when I was away racing at the World Championships in South Korea. There was, regretfully, no popping home for the birth, so I left Emily and went off to race for Great Britain with my teammates. In the middle of the night before our first race I was awoken by Emily's mum on the phone, telling me we had a beautiful baby girl and that this time everything had gone very smoothly. I remember standing in my underpants in the hotel corridor, a tear in my eye, feeling so far away from my family.

The next morning, I wasn't sure whether to tell my team mates, who were preparing to compete in the first race of the World Championships. It was a serious time for us, with twelve months of training behind us, and we needed to get it right. I didn't want to distract anyone with unnecessary news, news that not everyone might want to hear or even care about. Rowing is a team sport in body and mind, and small distractions can have big effects on a whole crew. Somehow word got out over breakfast and everyone was supportive. I was so relieved and felt, strangely, that it took the pressure off us as a crew. We could now concentrate on the racing ahead.

I finally met my daughter when she was ten days old after a horrendously slow journey home from South Korea. Bursting through the door on a late summer's afternoon, tired and bedraggled from the long journey, my heart was pounding – I was so excited. To my amazement everyone was asleep. Jasper sprawled out at one end of the sofa in the way only four year olds can, Emily curled up at the other end, desperately trying to catch up on ten days with very little sleep. There on the floor, wrapped up in a white blanket in a tiny basket, was my daughter, red faced and utterly content. It wasn't exactly the reception I'd been hoping for, but it really was quite emotional.

I still felt detached, however. It wasn't for another week after returning, when giving tiny Daisy a bath and she looked up into my eyes, that I felt the connection. With Jasper I'd been there every step of that painful (for Emily) way, and my child felt like mine. I'd missed that initial connection with Daisy – it was very strange as everyone in our extended family had met her before me. When the connection did finally arrive, I knew it was strong. Daisy is my daughter and I love her more than it's possible to explain.

Jesse Bear, our third child, was born while I was on a training camp in South Africa. The timing was a little unlucky, as he was booked in to arrive via C-section when I was home but he decided to make a break for it three days early. Of course, there wasn't much we could do about it. When Jesse was taking his very first tiny breaths of cool, fresh air, I was gasping for any air on a rowing machine in the sweatbox of our hotel gym with 25 other men. When I had requested to delay my training session so that I could wait by the phone to hear the news, Jürgen Gröbler replied, 'Alex, zere is nothing you can do. But maybe it will make you row faster?'

So that was that. The moment passed in an extremely undignified fashion – me, eight thousand miles away, dressed in Lycra, dripping with sweat. We now had three children.

Time is the one resource we can't buy but we all want. The appreciation of time is never more apparent than when bringing

My family, by Daisy. We all have big belly buttons and
very long toes!

until he was sick. At the time it felt like a disaster, but now we sit
around the dinner table and laugh about that together – and will
continue to do so for many years to come.

The possibilities are limitless out there, and it's often the first
step outside the front door that is the hardest. What children want
is time together, any time. Nothing has to be perfect for it to be
memorable. I hope you enjoy … Happy memory-making!

Alex, Emily, Jasper, Daisy and Jesse

AFTER-SCHOOL ADVENTURES

'Observation is a dying art.'

Stanley Kubrick

There's a period of time between the end of school and dinner time. It's a grey area, fuzzy and non-specific. There's a lot to do in these few hours ... but also nothing to do. Sometimes there's an after-school club that fills the time – multi-sports, football or tennis, or an art club at which your child paints a colourful mess on a thin piece of disintegrating paper, a masterpiece you've got to keep for years in a pile on a kitchen surface otherwise you're a bad parent. But some days there's nothing to do. Everyone is tired and hungry, and children are often bad-tempered from having had to rein in their emotions all day in the classroom.

It's all too tempting to go straight home, switch on the TV as you walk briskly through the house to the kitchen and flick the kettle on for your umpteenth coffee of the day. You need this coffee just to get you through the next few hours of the afternoon and into the evening. You spend two hours pottering around, tidying up, finishing off a bit of work, starting jobs you won't finish that evening, while the kids become lethargic and bored, watching nothing they'll remember on the TV. I should say here that watching TV is sometimes the right thing for them to do. There are some fantastic programmes for all ages on TV, and giving kids the opportunity after a busy day at school to rest on the sofa engrossed in an educational or fun programme is brilliant. But I'm also going to be honest – many of us do this far too much, as it's an easy escape from having to interact with your children when they might be in a difficult mood.

So what can we do? With a little bit of planning, these fuzzy grey hours can provide an opportunity to enjoy something truly productive and fun. I don't always get the chance to pick the kids up from school, but when I do I want to make it memorable for them. I think it's quite exciting for them when I pick them up because it's slightly unusual. 'Dad's here!' I hear the words drift over the mass of kids in front of me as I spot their beaming faces across the playground. While I was competing it was so unexpected for me to pick up Daisy from nursery that she'd burst into tears as soon as she saw me. I then had to head back out of the door and re-enter so she could prepare herself for my arrival! It's not the best feeling when your child bursts into tears at the sight of you, but I understand it.

This time of day provides a wonderful opportunity for our young people, so if you can, actually make the effort to arrive at the school gates with a plan already in place. It might be that your kids choose to go to school by scooter or bike, and you follow behind. If this is the case, tell them before you set off that day, that today is a walking day and they should leave their machines behind. It'll be hard at first, but they'll soon see the benefits!

There's always something to look at, something to point at, something out there to talk about. Whether it's why the wind is blowing in a certain direction, why the clouds look like they do, what plant is growing down there and how it can be used, or what creatures are living under that stone. So when walking back along the pavement from school or when strolling across the fields point things out, look up, down and all around. Ask questions, stimulate conversation and create intrigue. Nurture the inquiring mind so that it will grow to be interested – and interesting. Even the smallest thing that you might consider insignificant can be fascinating to young eyes. The trick is seeing it in the first place!

Quick inspiration

+ Make up an adventure story from the things you see
+ Point out five unusual things on the journey home
+ Talk about the weather
+ Identify an animal
+ Identify three trees

SIMPLE TREASURE HUNT

A treasure hunt is something very special and memorable. With a bit of planning it's easy to set up, whether in the garden, a local park or even along the street on the walk home from school. A little detour to do something interesting can really make the difference to a young person's day. This activity can be scaled up and turned into a long full-day adventure over a weekend or during the summer holidays. The longer it is, the more time is needed for planning, but the effort is certainly worth it. Don't forget a torch if you're planning a treasure hunt at night!

What you need

+ Pen and paper
+ Some planning time

What to do

1. Think about the route you'll take, either on the way back from school or once you get back home. As an example, give yourself 45 minutes to go around the block before dinner time. On your route there will be at least one of the following: a tree, a post box, a phone box, a loose rock and an old fence. Any noticeable features such as these are useful points towards which you can direct the budding treasure hunter.

2. Devise a clue for each location. An example might be: *'Leave the front door, take a turn to the east, find the next clue where nature's bombs hit the ground and grow.'*

3. Your child can figure out which way is east by using a compass or the position of the setting sun, and once they work out what 'nature's bombs' are they'll lead you to the conker tree at the corner of the street. There they'll search around excitedly under a pile of leaves or in the hollow of the tree where they'll find the

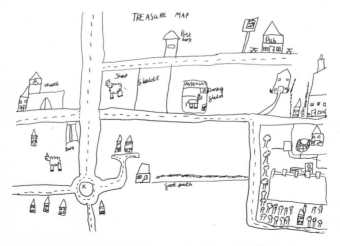

A treasure map of our village, by Jasper. X marks the spot — can you see it?

next clue you hid earlier in the day: *'Thirteen steps to the left and straight ahead, Postman Pat mustn't take the letter that's in the flower bed.'*

4. In the flower bed next to Postman Pat's letter box they'll find the next clue.

These are of course simple little clues I've thought up for the purposes of demonstration here. You'll have to adjust the clues depending on your children's age, interests and where you're holding the treasure hunt. There don't have to be many clues, and the hunt doesn't have to take a long time for it to become a fun outdoors activity that you do together. As a parent, it's fantastic to watch your child work things out, get frustrated and then enjoy the fruits of their efforts by discovering the route and eventual goal. It's also a wonderfully bonding experience … but be prepared. Once you've created your first treasure hunt, your child will demand many more. So get thinking about those clues!

SCAVENGER HUNT

What you need

+ Compass
+ Tin foil
+ Metal detector
+ Camera
+ Map
+ Plastic collection bags/sandwich bags

What to do

1. Provide approximate distances (in child's paces, 'lengths' of a school playing field or similar, or metres) and compass directions to follow to get to the point at which the next clue is hidden.

2. Wrap objects in tin foil and hide them in the ground, under leaves or under non-metallic objects for your child to find with their metal detector. This could be a prize or the next clue.

3. Set challenges of things outside that they have to photograph along the scavenger-hunt route. Only when they've correctly found, identified and photographed all the items you've listed do they receive the next clue or prize.

4. Set them a route to follow on a map. Maps are wonderful things and map-reading a brilliant skill to grasp early on. They are fascinating pictorial views of the countryside, and learning the symbols and markings is great fun. Setting a route together and allowing your child to take you along the route is a hugely rewarding experience.

5. Set the route based on items they can collect. Leaves, interesting stones, wood, tree bark, pine cones can all be collected in a bag. If all the items have been correctly identified and collected they have successfully completed the scavenger hunt.

Using a combination of some or all of these ideas you can create an incredibly interesting, exciting and varied scavenger hunt, in which your child has to use their brain as much as their energy in order to complete it!

Challenge

As you and your child become increasingly accustomed to the process of a scavenger hunt you can start adding in extra components to make the hunt even more exciting. Switching between a clue they have to work out, a clue or item they have to find, even a challenge they have to complete before you give them another clue, is a great way to extend and enhance this game.

> *My dad was a master of treasure hunts. For years my birthday parties would involve long hunts over miles and miles of countryside. Up and down hills, across fields, along rivers, up trees and straight through woods. A clue or riddle would lead to the next point, and so on until we eventually found the prize. This would sometimes take all day to complete. His clever little cryptic clues were difficult but we always managed to get a hint out of him as he followed on behind, sending us off in the right direction. It was so much fun and such a thrilling way to spend the day.*

FLOUR/SAWDUST TRAIL

A flour or sawdust treasure trail is a simple activity, and a great way to get kids outdoors and active. Either as a high-energy exercise done at speed with a teenager or at a slower pace with the family as a whole, it is a fantastic way to encourage movement and can be such a good laugh. As with the treasure or scavenger hunt, it can turn into a long full-day undertaking, but it's also perfect to use up the last of the day's energy after school, or even in the dark with a torch.

What you need

+   A bag of flour or sawdust

What to do

With younger kids who can't be left alone, set up the trail in advance. It doesn't have to be long, but again the beauty of this is that it can be done in both urban and rural settings.

1. Every 5 to 10 metres drop a small pile of flour or sawdust to mark a trail for your child to follow. This can be on the edge of a path, on a tree branch, on a wall or piled in any other place that is not immediately obvious.
2. Make sure you mix up the location of the flour or sawdust to keep the difficulty up and interest going. If you discover it's too easy for them, then next time use bigger gaps between drops so they have to really search and even double back on themselves.
3. Be thoughtful of where other people will walk, so avoid dropping flour or sawdust right in the centre of a busy pavement or anywhere it will look unsightly.
4. Allow yourself a 10-minute head start and make your way off along the route, dropping a small amount of flour or sawdust at regular intervals.
5. Your kids will race after you at top speed following your trail with intent. With the head start, you've given yourself time to create false paths and decoys, where you can double back on yourself and continue along the correct route. When you've come to the end of the intended route, why not hide and wait for them? Climb high into the branches of a tree and sit watching their progress as they approach the tree you've led them to and

the trail runs cold. Eventually they'll think to look up, where you'll be waiting.

6. This is an active challenge that stimulates thought and observation. Watching your child work out problems, see the next clue, charge after it and on to the next is hugely satisfying and great fun! We always bring the hunt back round in a loop to our house, where dinner will be waiting or where there's a hidden chocolate prize that can be eaten for dessert.

Challenge

How about creating a trail that finishes at a pub where you can all have dinner together, or ending the trail at a perfect site to start a little fire to cook some marshmallows over? There doesn't always have to be a prize. The fact that you're doing something together is the prize – all that kids really want is time with you.

SHELTER WITH A HOT DRINK

This simple activity can be done anywhere and can turn a boring trip home from school into a fun little memorable experience. The beauty of this is that it can be done whatever the weather – in fact it often works best when the weather's at its worst!

What you need

+ A flask of your preferred hot drink and some non-breakable cups
+ A large plastic sheet/tarpaulin

What to do

1. Take a flask containing your hot drink with you on the school pick-up, along with a large plastic sheet or tarpaulin. It's even better if it's raining because there will be fewer people out, making it even more exciting.
2. If going by car, find a spot to stop and park up. The verge at the edge of a field or next to a park or playing field is ideal.
3. Hunker down against the hedge or under a tree, sitting on the plastic sheet and pulling it up over your backs to keep out the weather and create a small, dry shelter.

4. You'll soon warm up in there, especially while sharing a warm drink. It's your time to be together, talking and watching what goes on outside when everyone else heads for home. It's also a chance to watch the wildlife that stays out feeding in the rain and watch the passers-by, too, although they probably won't even notice you there. It's an opportunity to enjoy time together in, let's face it, a very unusual place!

This activity is so basic, so simple and doesn't cost a thing – and yet I expect 99 per cent of people reading this have never done it.

I first did something similar with Daisy in the summer when she had just started nursery. We stopped on the way home from pick-up and bought an ice cream each. Having a whole ice cream herself at that time in her life was a real treat, so she was already excited and happy. It happened to be a beautifully warm summer's afternoon, and as I parked the car on the edge of a field close to home, overlooking the crops swaying in the breeze, we both knew this would be a good moment. Daisy and I sat on the bonnet of my car looking over the landscape and enjoying our ice creams, and we certainly weren't expecting what was to happen next.

We started to see ladybirds flying all around us. As we noticed them landing on us, more and more appeared until the air was thick with these little red and black bugs. They covered my car, flew on to our clothes, into our hair and all over us. We were amazed, gobsmacked by this little event happening around us. It really was a sudden natural phenomenon. I assume we had parked in the path of a swarm moving across the fields. They were possibly descending on the crops to feed on greenfly and we just happened to be right in their path.

The point I want to make is that Daisy still talks about that 40 minutes we spent in the field with our ice creams and the ladybirds.

If we hadn't made the effort to stop, we wouldn't have experienced that natural event. It's only a small thing and it didn't take long, but it's a lasting memory for Daisy and me. We treasure that event, one that won't ever happen in exactly the same way again. But next time, maybe something different will!

The funny thing is, when we really need to do this sort of thing we just don't. As an adult, doing something out of the norm when you're at your most stressed is usually the very last thing you'll want to do, even though it's usually the time you need to do it the most. That first step out the door is the hardest thing, but once you've taken it you realise its value. I hope my children still want to do this with me when they are teenagers. I have a sneaking suspicion that they will.

SET AN INSECT TRAP

I've always been fascinated by insects and indeed would go so far as to say I love them. They're incredible creatures that thrive all over the world, sometimes in the most hostile environments, and are the most diverse and ecologically important group of land animals. Nobody knows exactly how many different insects there are, although it's estimated there are as many 30 million different species of these weird and wonderful creatures. One of the most useful things about them is that they're absolutely everywhere. You can always find an insect, and so wherever you are in the world there's entertainment to be had. In a city centre, leaning against a wall or waiting by a bus stop with a hedge behind you – have a look, peer into the undergrowth or between the cracks in a crumbling wall, as there's always something there to spot.

A group of insects we collected, by Jasper. I'm pleased he
believes they're all smiling.

An easy way to discover what you have in your garden, front yard,
local park or woodland is to set a small insect trap. It's quick to make
and costs nothing except time.

What you need

+ A glass jar or clear beaker
+ Some bait
+ A small spade
+ One large, flat rock
+ Three small rocks

What to do

1. Find a spot on the ground in a place where people don't usually walk. Under a rock in a flower bed is a great place to start, or in a quiet corner of the garden.
2. Dig a hole as deep as the glass jar or beaker.
3. Place your bait in the jar or beaker and then put it in the hole and adjust it so the top of the jar is in line with the surface of the soil or just a fraction below.
4. Compact the soil around the top.
5. Place the three small rocks around the embedded jar on the soil surface and carefully place the large flat rock on top of them to prevent rain getting in. You're done!
6. The trap is set. Now leave it alone for a few hours or, ideally, overnight.
7. Check the traps the following morning.

This is a great activity to do on a Friday afternoon after school, providing a perfect and exciting pretext for getting up and out on a weekend. If you're organised, you can get a whole load of traps set in different parts of the garden, park or woodland – wherever you

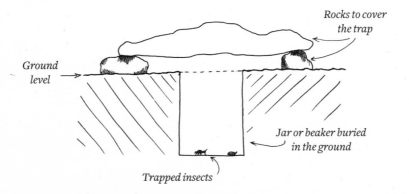

Rocks to cover the trap

Ground level

Jar or beaker buried in the ground

Trapped insects

have easy access. It's interesting to put a range of food in the jar or beaker to see what it attracts. Different bait will draw different insects, but even if you don't use a food source, you'll catch something. Also try to notice which insects live in the habitat where you set your traps. Grassland, for example, is likely to contain different species to woodland.

Muddy hands, dirty knees, fresh air and fun together. And don't forget to return the insects back where you found them.

Challenge

I'd suggest taking a white tray or bowl so that you can study your trapped insects. Once you've pulled the jar or beaker from the ground and had a good look through the glass, tip out your finds into the tray or bowl to have a further look from a different angle. The light white enables the usually dark insects to show up really well. From there you'll be able to talk about them, identify them and maybe, if you're all in the mood or have the time, draw and photograph them.

Talking points

+   How many legs?
+   Colour?
+   Shape?
+   Texture?
+   Speed?

MAKE AN INSECT ASPIRATOR

Taking insect collecting even further, how about making an aspirator? An aspirator is a clever little device that enables you to suck through one pipe, drawing air and, hopefully, an insect through another. The way it's made means you won't be able to suck the insect into your mouth – as long as you get the tubes the right way round it's a very safe way to collect your insect treasure. You can buy pre-made aspirators online, but they're just as fun to make and test out as they are to use outdoors for real. I've made some with my kids, and it's a really engrossing practical activity that gets you all thinking. And, what's more, you see the results immediately.

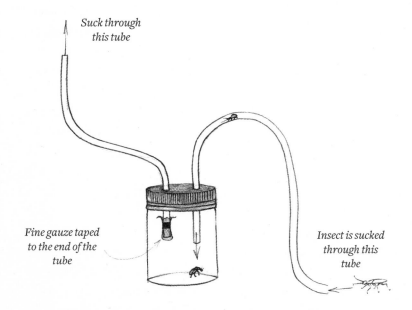

Suck through this tube

Fine gauze taped to the end of the tube

Insect is sucked through this tube

What you need

+ A flexible plastic tube, around 45cm long. Aquarium tube is perfect. Alternatively, thick drinking straws can also work.
+ A small, clear plastic container with a lid – jam-jar size is large enough.
+ A piece of fine gauze around 4cm square. Any fine material that allows air to flow freely through can be used.
+ Tape. Electrical, duct tape or Sellotape all work well.

What to do

1. Cut the plastic tube into two equal lengths.
2. Very carefully pierce a hole in the lid of the plastic container. The hole needs to allow one end of the tube to fit in without gaps around the aperture. Push one length of the tube through, leaving approximately 15cm of tube protruding from the lid of the container.
3. Pierce another hole in the lid, in exactly the same way, next to the first.
4. Wrap the piece of gauze around the end of the second length of tube and secure with tape. You should be able to freely suck on the non-gauze end of the tube.
5. Push the second tube, gauze first, in through the second hole you made in the container lid, ensuring there are no gaps around the tube. Again, approximately 15cm of tube should protrude from the lid of the container.
6. Take your aspirator outside and go insect hunting.
7. Using an aspirator is simple, but do make sure you help your child remember which tube is the correct tube to suck by marking the suck tube with a piece of tape. You must always

suck in through the tube with the gauze covering one end, otherwise you're likely to get a mouthful of insects!

8. When you uncover a rock or part the grass to find an interesting-looking insect, take the aspirator down to the ground.

9. Holding the tube (without the gauze) over the insect, suck through the other tube (with gauze). As long as you're close enough to the insect, it will be sucked up through the tube into the container and left to rest at the bottom. It will be trapped until you let it out.

You can collect insects easily, quickly and safely by this method. It's great fun but quite nerve-wracking, as it takes a little bit of time to get used to the fact that you won't suck the insects up into your mouth. Together, you can quickly amass a wonderful collection of small insects without harming them, and if your container is clear you can inspect them easily.

Challenge

As with the insect trap, it's worth taking a white bowl or tray outside with you so that viewing your insects is easier once they've been collected in the aspirator. We always try to identify the insects we find together and read a little bit about them, in this way slowly developing our knowledge of insects.

Once you have inspected, photographed, identified and studied the collected insects, make sure you always return them to the place from were they were collected. It's important to show we don't have ownership over the life around us, and that includes looking after what we find and returning it to where it belongs.

I clearly remember the first aspirator that was bought for me as a child. I was incredibly excited – but nervous about using it. I guess I didn't take enough care, so a couple of times I ended up with beetles and ants in the back of my throat. It gives you a shock, but they are little more than a taste of protein!

MAKE STRING

Creating something with your own hands is extremely rewarding. Of course, in times past there was no choice but to make everything you needed, but no one can realistically do so now. With this activity it's not so much about the product you make – let's be honest, the string you make simply isn't going to be as good as any you can buy in a shop – but the process of making it from material you find is rewarding and great fun. When sitting there making it, watching the string grow longer, you really feel a great sense of satisfaction.

What you need

+   A good supply of strong, natural fibres. Raffia is the best and easiest to use. It's a very strong fibre that's been prepared perfectly, ready for you to create your string. Garden centres, florists and craft shops often sell packets very cheaply for tying up plants and displaying flowers, and one packet is sufficient for you to make metres of thin string. Flax fibres are ideal, too.
+   It's also possible to make string with stinging-nettle stems, very fine tree roots or the bark of certain species of tree, such

as willow, cut into thin strips. All these will take a little extra processing to get into the thin strands required.

+   Strong fingers and patience.

What to do

1. Find a comfortable place to sit.
2. Gather a few long fibres together between your fingers and find the middle point of all the fibres.
3. Bend them in half to get to the starting point of your string.
4. Hold the bend of the fibres firmly between the fingers of one hand and in the fingers of your other hand twist the top fibres together.
5. As you twist, pull them around and underneath the bottom fibres, and hold in position.
6. Take the fibres that are now at the top and repeat the movement, twisting and pulling around the back. These first few moves are the most tricky. From here on the process is simple and you'll find yourself developing an easy rhythm.
7. You'll be alternating which group of fibres are at the top. Each time twist them tightly, then move them around the back and repeat.
8. It's important to keep the strands tight and the twists close together. This will make your string much stronger and more useable. In no time at all you'll see your skills working and a piece of string will form.
9. Nature does a pretty good job but, unfortunately, it doesn't produce never-ending fibres, so you'll soon get to the end of your fibres. When this happens it's a really simple process to add in more fibres so you can continue to make a longer piece of string.

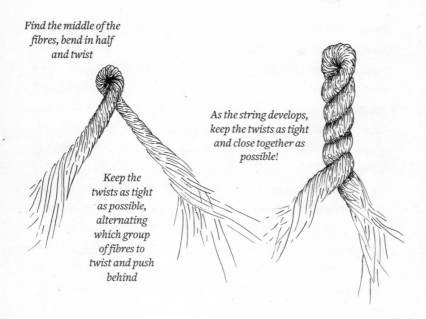

Find the middle of the fibres, bend in half and twist

As the string develops, keep the twists as tight and close together as possible!

Keep the twists as tight as possible, alternating which group of fibres to twist and push behind

10. Take two more long fibres, bend them in half and at the bend push them into the point where your string is coming together.
11. As tightly as you can, continue the process, now twisting and turning these new fibres as well as the old.
12. It's important to keep the new pieces tight in, with no gaps where they meet the original fibres.
13. Continue until you have made the length of string you want.
14. Once you have made as much as you want to, simply gather all the strands together and tie a knot in the end. Cut away the remaining strands of fibre past the knot to neaten it up.

Ropes for ships used to be made out of hemp like this in times past. It must have been painstaking work, but the twisting and turning back on itself produces an incredibly strong cord. The tighter the twists you make, the stronger the string will be.

I was first taught how to make string by a relative of mine. He and his wife turned up at our house one afternoon in a battered, old red postal van that had been converted inside to become their home. They were nomads from Australia on a journey around the world, selling products that they'd made themselves, notably tiny little crepe-paper kites. These kites really did work incredibly well too! We spent the afternoon together, and I was drawn in and fascinated by the skills of this guy.

He'd been adopted by an Aborigine mother and brought up in the bush, so from a very young age he'd been taught bushcraft – how to survive by living off the land and making things. Once he'd shown me how to construct one of these little kites, I'd learnt to play (badly) the didgeridoo and the pheasant he'd picked up on the way to us had been 'processed' (I'm fairly sure it was roadkill), we then started work on making string.

Digging out a supply of dried flax grass from a corner of the van, he proceeded to show me the way to hold the fibres, twist, push away, turn, pinch and repeat. Before my eyes, the most perfect piece of natural string I've ever seen grew between his tough, leathery, supple, skilled fingers. Very quickly he'd made a foot-long length of string, and as he twisted and turned he talked to me about all things outdoors and living out of the back of a van. As this amazing product was made he showed me how to make it thicker and thinner for different requirements. I was transfixed.

We've always used string made this way for bracelets and necklaces. Turning it into a bracelet is simplicity itself. Once you've made a knot in one end, simply wrap the string around your wrist and push the knot through the twist at the start of your piece of string. Because it's been twisted tight, the knot will hold tight, forming a secure bracelet around your wrist. My daughter Daisy makes them for me now, and I love wearing her rough little bracelets, as they remind me of

the effort she's taken to fashion them, the skill she's learnt from me
in doing so and the time we've spent outside, quietly making
them together.

USE A PENKNIFE

Using a knife is exceedingly simple, but for young children it
certainly requires guidance. Strangely, on balance, I'd say the sharper
the knife, the safer it is for the kinds of jobs for which we require a
knife in the outdoors. But this comes at a cost – if the blade comes in
contact with skin, then the cut will most likely be more significant.
Care must be taken at all times. But if you follow the guidelines
below, your child should be safe.

What you need

+   A sharp penknife

What to do

1. Hold your knife firmly in your writing hand, creating a strong,
   comfortable position.
2. Always push the blade in a direction away from your body. Your
   child will always be tempted to push it in other directions –
   towards their torso, hands or legs – but be very strict with
   them to start with. This is the single-most important rule
   regarding knife use and it must be drummed in from the
   outset.

3. Give them a simple task to start with, such as carving the top of a walking stick (see 'Make a walking stick', page 39).

4. Encourage them to finish off their small project by sanding the wood they've whittled. Seeing the transformation of a piece of rough driftwood or scrap wood into a smooth, beautiful piece, where the grain of the wood shows up strong and clear, is a fascinating phenomenon and will show them a wonder of the natural world.

Challenge

We can't all be on the go all the time. Woodcarving or whittling is a wonderful, relaxing activity you can do outdoors together with your child. If you both have a penknife you can head outside, find a quiet spot with a good view and sit carving a piece of wood together. Ideas for projects include carving a small boat, tiny animals, a walking stick, a wooden spoon or a face in a log. The ideas are endless and the activity is restful, peaceful, creative and fun.

My grandfather would always carry a knife around with him. It was a part of him, just as much as his trousers or any other item of his clothing. His knives weren't anything special – just silver folding gardeners' penknives – but he'd always have one attached to his belt by a lanyard. I'd watch him swiftly pull it from his pocket while out in the garden to cut a bit of orange binder twine, trim a tree branch, whittle a spike on a stick to push into the ground to support a tree, butter his bread or cut a piece of cheese.

I grew up wanting to have something that was so useful always on me, just like he did. Unfortunately he wasn't so good at remembering he was carrying a knife in airports, with the result that he had his knives taken off him a couple of times when flying somewhere on holiday. Of course, he argued it was his favourite knife, he'd had it for years and would they please post it back to him? Alas, that particular trusty penknife was never seen again, but as soon as he returned from holiday he'd buy a replacement. I longed for one of those silver knives, with a locking mechanism and a piece of string with which I could tie it on to my trousers. I couldn't ever work out where he was buying these knives. None of the shops I ever went into sold them.

My dad owned a garden centre and for a long time I thought that he didn't stock these most essential gardeners' knives. Then one day, one very memorable day, browsing the shelves in his shop I spotted the Holy Grail. There, on a shelf, encased within a shiny plastic packet, was my grandfather's penknife. I was 10 years old and desperate for the heavenly tool I saw before me. Thinking quickly, I debated whether this would be my first robbery. It was my dad's shop, I spent most of my weekends there and it was like my home. Surely, I reasoned, it wasn't too bad taking something you really wanted from your own home. I'd taken the odd Calippo ice lolly from the freezer when no one was looking, but somehow this felt different, much more serious. I put the packet back on the shelf and walked sadly away. Of course I wouldn't steal a penknife.

It was a long couple of months after discovering that dad stocked that knife that I was given one of my very own. I must have pestered him relentlessly, every day going to that part of the shop and looking dreamily at the packet. Dad eventually relented and gave me my first knife lesson with my own *penknife. His lesson was simple: always cut away from you. That was it. That was all I needed to know. Naturally, I've had to learn the hard way, but when you make your first mistake with your knife you learn pretty quickly.*

Having my own penknife, tied to my belt on a lanyard gave me a feeling of responsibility, one I valued very much, and I felt that it

*was a big step in my parents trusting me with something important.
I couldn't wait to show it to my grandfather. As soon as the summer
holidays came we drove down to Devon to his farm and we were soon
comparing knives. His was well used – for real reasons, unlike mine,
which had been used to cut a bit of paper just to check it was still sharp
as hell, or to pierce the tiniest of holes in my T-shirt, again, just to
check. We quickly got to work whittling sticks, cutting rope, buttering
our bread. I still have that knife today.*

*As a 10-year-old boy it's not exactly practical to carry a penknife
attached to the belt of your trousers. Teachers at school don't look
altogether favourably on that. Children shouldn't carry knives unless
they are properly and sensibly supervised at all times by an adult.
For Jasper's eighth birthday I bought him his first penknife and he
was thrilled. It's a special kids' one with a rounded end to avoid any
unwanted accidents, but the blade itself is just as sharp as any adult
knife. We're starting to use it together for tasks we do outside, like
carving a spoon to use to eat outdoors, cut some chopsticks, make a
whistle, gather tinder for a fire and create sparks to light it, and so
many other things. It's really important to show a young child, within
reason, the values and dangers of a knife. I learnt its value as a tool
from observing my grandfather over the years. Using a knife is fun, but
it's definitely not a toy. A knife really must be respected.*

MAKE A WALKING STICK

One of the quickest things you can do in the countryside is make a walking stick, a simple item that can be treasured and used for years to come. There's no point finding a rotten old branch that will snap as soon as it's used as a pole to vault across a puddle or stream. No, you need to be making walking sticks that can withstand the rigours of a life outdoors. If you're lucky enough to live in the countryside a short distance from some woods or a hedgerow then it'll be easy to find the materials you need. Alternatively, there are resources online that can provide suitable natural materials. Failing that, a perfect walking stick, if cut to size, can be made from a broom handle bought from any hardware store. OK, you won't be finding the raw materials yourself, but you can still adapt, adjust and alter as desired.

When you and your child spend time preparing this stick, they will care. They'll become attached to it, and, in turn, they'll want to use it. They'll start asking to go out for a walk with their stick. Hopefully, they'll remind you to bring it to the school pick-up so that after school they have their adventure equipment ready. Making the stick is an adventure in itself.

What you need

+ A stick that's taller than your child
+ A saw/pair of secateurs
+ A penknife

What to do

1. It's important to get permission from whoever's land your stick is growing on.
2. Keep your eyes peeled for long, straight poles growing up from the ground.
3. Hazel is the best species of tree to look for, but ash, blackthorn and holly are all suitable too.
4. Coppicing is a method of woodland management employed by woodsmen who require long, straight poles. When tree stems attain a certain diameter – an inch or two – they are cut at ground level and used for hedging or charcoal production. The tree stump then sprouts again, sending up new, straight poles. Woodsmen can choose the thickness of the pole, depending on the requirements they have, leaving some to grow for many years while others can be cut after just a few.
5. Hazel is the most commonly coppiced tree. Coppicing is a sustainable method of producing wood. Hazel can easily be found in woodland or hedges, and usually provides a range of diameters to fit any size of hand. Hazel is easily cut and carved, and is very flexible, making it ideal for walking sticks.
6. Depending on the age of your child, adjust the size of stick you choose. Thinner lengths for younger children will be lighter and more easily handled; slightly thicker, more robust sticks will be better for older children, who will be more likely to put their weight on the wood.
7. Once you've found the perfect-sized piece of wood carefully cut the pole from the base. The leaves and any twigs growing off can be removed to create a beautifully smooth, straight stick.

Cutting their own walking stick can be a wonderful lesson for your child. Give them the saw and show them trust, but it's vital that you show them how to use any tools safely. If they are involved in every aspect of this process they'll appreciate, learn and remember so much more. When the final draw of the saw cuts through the stick it's an incredibly satisfying achievement for a young child and one that should be celebrated.

Now you have your walking stick – poking stick, wizard's staff, pole-vault pole or whatever else it is you've decided to use it for – you can head out into the world with a tool that you have sourced, made into something useful and worked on together.

LADYBIRD WALKING STICK

You now have a simple walking stick that your child is already hopefully pleased with. Walking has suddenly become easier and more enjoyable. Now it's time to create something really fun using a number of different skills.

What you need

+   A cut walking stick
+   A penknife
+   Acrylic paints (red and black)

What to do

1. With a penknife, start carving the top of the walking stick into the shape of a ball.

2. Depending on the type of wood you've found, the shaving of the end should be fairly easy with a sharp penknife. Again, fresh hazel is ideal.

3. This is the perfect activity for you to teach your child safe-knife technique (see 'Use a penknife', page 35). You're not making anything complicated, so the cutting of the wood can be done all in the same direction, making this an ideal exercise with a knife.

4. Once you have a smooth, rounded end to your walking stick, it's time to get out the paints.

5. This part can be as simple or as complicated as you want to make it. We've always kept it really simple and just dipped the rounded end into some good red acrylic paint.

6. Leave this to dry, which does take a little while. Perhaps it's now time for dinner!

7. Finish it off by turning the little red ball on the end of the stick into a ladybird. All that's needed is black paint – or even a black Sharpie – to give you a line straight down the middle, some small eyes and a load of black dots.

A ladybird looks really great on the end of the stick, turning the walking stick into something even more special, something cut, carved, painted and cared for by you and your child. As an after-school activity it's perfect. It doesn't take too long, it's engrossing, and there's something at the end of it all that will be used and treasured for a long while to come.

If the stick gets damaged, broken or lost it's no problem. There's barely any cost and it gives you the opportunity to do it all over again. I promise you your ladybird artwork will improve in time too!

We've given these simple hand-crafted products as presents to people in the past. Without fail, people love the design and the thought – and they use them! Whether you're an adult or a child, if you receive one of these walking sticks you'll be dead chuffed. Of course, it doesn't have to be a ladybird on the end; it could be anything, although the simple ball shape is easy to carve out. Have a go at carving other things from the wood and adding carved designs down the stick too. The options are limitless, and as your carving skills are practised and developed your sticks will only get better. Before long, like at ours, there will be a whole collection of sticks of different lengths, thicknesses and questionable designs at your front door.

READ SOMEWHERE UNUSUAL

If your lives are anything like ours, getting the evening school-book reading done is not the easiest thing in the world. We're finding more and more that reading is left until the last moment before we walk out of the house in the morning. It always seems to be done in a rush, with a toothbrush in the mouth and everyone scrambling around to find what they need for the day. This is not conducive to good concentration and therefore enjoyable reading time. It's certainly tricky with three children, giving each one the time they need and deserve. It's something we're always battling with and trying to figure out.

What you need

+ A reading book/homework
+ Warm clothes
+ A rug or coat to sit on
+ Tarpaulin or plastic sheet to shelter under

What to do

1. Take your child to read or do their homework somewhere unusual after school, anywhere that isn't home.

Daisy and Daddy sitting under a hedge reading, by Daisy. Notice the smile – they are genuine from us both.

2. Stop somewhere with a good view – run up a hill or climb a tree, walk to the middle of a field or clamber into a den you've made.
3. Take a large plastic sheet or tarpaulin and shelter underneath it in the dry and read together when it's bad weather.

Despite being outside with plenty to look at and with it being a strange situation, it's actually really easy to concentrate. For some reason, taking yourselves away from the everyday distractions of home concentrates the mind and enables you to focus on what you're doing. I've found that Jasper remembers the books or parts of the books that he's read in unusual places far more than he does when at home. If the book doesn't get read, then at least you've spent some time together outdoors that you wouldn't otherwise have done. So it's a win-win!

CLIMB A BEANSTALK

The story of 'Jack and the Beanstalk' has grabbed all our imaginations at some point in our lives. We've all been nervous for Jack as he climbs skywards towards the land of the giant at the top of the beanstalk, and yet more scared when he hides from this behemoth of a man, shouting weird and scary words at the top of his lungs. What does 'Fee-fi-fo-fum' even mean? There have been many versions of the story written over the years, with various different illustrations, all creating fear and excitement in those who hear it. After school, to use up that last bit of energy in your young person, why not climb to the top of the beanstalk and encourage them to catch the giant!

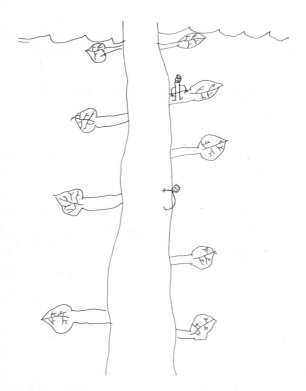

Climbing a beanstalk, by Jasper. Sometimes the giant is scary,
sometimes he's nice, but he always makes us laugh.

Suitable trees aren't always available at short notice with limited
time, but if they are, then great. Helping your child escape and create
a game in an imaginary world is stimulating and hugely beneficial.

What you need

+ A climbing tree with plenty of branches low down, so your child
  can get off the ground.

What to do

1. This activity is like a game of hide and seek, but it's more exciting. Have an idea of a tree you can climb into and be prepared to run.
2. Ask your child to count up to an agreed number.
3. As with hide and seek, quickly make your way to the tree and climb to a point that's just out of their reach. If they can climb, then the higher the better. If they're too young to climb, it's no problem. Just get slightly off the ground. This could be on a stool, a garden bench, a big rock or a tree stump. Once they finish counting and start looking, the fun begins.
4. When they spot you up in the tree, start acting like a giant, growling 'Fee-fi-fo-fum' and swinging the branches.
5. The game stops when they reach you and touch your feet.

It's such a simple activity but incorporates so much. It gives you and your child the chance to be free, run and climb. I guarantee there will be a lot of laughter when the game is in full swing.

Please do take care, as an excited child climbing a tree can pose dangers. In the excitement to catch you they can forget to hold on. Please be aware of this as you play the game.

Challenge

Change the character who has to be found. You could be a pirate, dinosaur, monster, alien or an escaped wild animal from the zoo.

Guarding treasure is a great game. Take a piece of cloth that is the treasure. Tie it loosely at the place you have climbed to. Once you're caught, they've won the treasure and get to go and hide and guard it themselves.

CLOUD SPOTTING

Much of what we do involves looking down. We look down to read,
write, watch animals, find insects, build dens, carve wood, start
fires and cook. When you think about it, we don't spend much time
looking upwards into the sky. But the sky is ever-changing. It's a
dynamic space of swirling particles and molecules. Skies change
colour and shape all the time, and so to have a very basic knowledge
about the sky can mean that looking at it is much more interesting.
If you know what you're seeing you'll notice things more. When
you notice things more, you'll become more interested in those
things and want to learn more about them. When you know more

Cloud spotting, by Jasper. Jasper watches the clouds in the sky —
amazingly, he's got the dog doing it too.

about them, you'll want to share your knowledge with others, which sustains this ever-growing cycle of interest and knowledge.

The sky is a mystery to children, and the source of endless stimulation to their imagination. As we grow older, our heads grow heavier and our eyes become diverted towards the ground. Why not have a go at changing that, and turning your own and your children's heads to the sky?

What you need

+ Eyes!

What to do

1. Go outside, tilt your head to the sky and open your eyes.
2. This can be done any and every time you're outside, whether you're in the countryside or in the heart of a bustling city. Look up out of the car window or, even better, stop, get out of the car, lean up against it and look up. If you're not too worried about the paintwork then why not spread a picnic mat on the car roof and allow your child to lie on their back and watch the sky.

What will you see?

+ *Cirrus*. These are the highest-forming clouds at 20,000–40,000 feet of altitude. I always think they look like wispy floating feathers high in the upper atmosphere. They are formed when warmer dry air rises, turning moisture into ice crystals, and they indicate a change in weather, where warmer air is moving in on a front.

+ *Cirrocumulus*. Also seen at 20,000–40,000 feet. These are sheets of clouds made up from small cloudlets of ice and they might cover large areas of the sky, looking like fish scales or ripples. These distinctive shapes are made when turbulent vertical currents of air meet a cirrus layer. They often indicate a change for the worse in the weather.

+ *Cirrostratus*. These white, often transparent, thin wisps of cloud are the thinnest you'll see. They can be used to predict the weather over the next 24 hours. They usually indicate that there's likely to be wet weather on the way – either persistent rain or sometimes only a light drizzle, depending on the specific qualities of the cloud.

+ *Altocumulus*. These are mid-layer clouds made up of water droplets and ice, giving them an ethereal appearance, and are usually white or grey. They differ from cirrocumulus, which are white, higher up and generally smaller.

+ *Altostratus*. Usually featureless, these are thin sheets of cloud stretching out over the entire sky. Sometimes the sun shows weakly through them. They usually form when a thin layer of cirrostratus drops from a higher level, and they can indicate that a change of the weather is on its way. They often form ahead of a warm front; as the front passes, the altostratus layer will deepen to form nimbostratus, which will produce rain or snow.

+ *Nimbostratus*. These are dark, grey featureless layers of cloud thick enough to block out most of the sun. The rain or snow they bring will usually remain until the front has moved on.

+ *Stratocumulus*. These are the most common clouds seen at low levels in the sky and have clear, defined bases. They are indicators of a change in the weather, but can be found in all types of weather, from settled, dry weather to rain.

+ *Stratus*. These are the lowest-lying type of cloud, uniform white or grey, which we know from dull, overcast days. They sometimes appear on the ground as mist or fog. They can produce light drizzle if thick enough.
+ *Cumulus*. If a child were to draw a cloud, it would be a cumulus cloud. They are detached, individual cauliflower-shaped clouds that form when warm air from the surface rises and cools to form water vapour, which then condenses and forms cloud. If they continue to grow in height and size they'll eventually turn into cumulonimbus clouds. Cumulus clouds indicate fair weather, but if they do grow into cumulonimbus clouds they are capable of producing rain.
+ *Cumulonimbus*. Everyone knows the look of these clouds. To me they are magnificent, exciting, daunting cathedrals of water vapour towering up into the sky. These thunderclouds are the only type of cloud that can produce thunder, lightning and hail. Their bases can lie very close to the Earth's surface but stretch high into the atmosphere. They often grow from small cumulus clouds over a hot ground surface and can also form along cold fronts where warm air is forced to rise over incoming cold air. They are associated with extreme weather and once precipitation begins, they'll usually only last a short period of time.

I studied physical geography at university, and weather was a part of the degree I remember enjoying very much. University for me was more about fitting lectures and study around rowing training, but because the subject was of genuine interest to me I managed to learn a significant amount. Now it's my job to pass that knowledge on to my children, which I try to do every time we go outside and I tell them to look up.

Challenge

As you're directing your gaze up to the sky, have a look to see if you can see anything in the shapes and patterns of the clouds. Most of the time, with the right cloud conditions, there's something obvious that can be made out from the shapes that form up there. Usually it's a strange creature or a face – let your imagination run wild!

There are a number of really useful apps and websites available for identifying cloud types. The more you look and compare the clouds, the easier it will become to distinguish between them. Of course, there are cross-overs and similar-looking clouds. They aren't always easy to identify, but it's great fun trying!

Give your child a mission to photograph the sky every day for a week. At the weekend collate all the photographs and identify them together, creating your own cloud-spotters' guide. It may take a number of weeks to get a wide range of different clouds, as they are obviously weather dependent.

COLLECT AND COOK SOME DINNER

This time after school is limited, bordered by a pretty restrictive schedule. Dinner time and bedtime in our house are relatively unmovable markers in the day, so why not make use of the time by collecting food and helping to prepare for the evening meal in an exciting and fun way.

Depending on the season, this could be really very simple or it may need a little extra planning. I admit that you wouldn't want to do this every day, but on occasion it can transform this grey, fuzzy period into a really fun, memorable activity. There are so many different plants, fruits, nuts and berries that are readily available, free, delicious and healthy, and out there. It's important to make sure you know exactly what it is you're collecting before you pick it, so check time and time again if you're not absolutely certain. Here I'm keeping it really simple, giving you a few options throughout the year.

What to do

1. Take a walk, always keeping an eye on the plants and trees around you.
2. It's important to be observant. The more observant you and your child are, the more you'll start to notice the often subtle differences between the various species that grow in your neighbourhood.
3. Always be willing to stop, look, check. Take your time.
4. Collect only the amount that you'll need.
5. Never touch any plant or mushroom that is – or could be – poisonous. If in any doubt at all, leave it alone.

SPRING

Spring is a beautiful time of the year. When people are asked for their favourite season, the answer is often spring. Perhaps we are experiencing a feeling that takes us back to the distant past, when winters really were something we had to struggle and fight through in order to even see the following year. Of course, very few of us these days really need to 'survive' the winter, but the feeling lives on.

Things start to grow because of the warmer temperatures and increased hours of daylight. Wildlife is active, and birds in particular are noticeably more active, preparing nests in which to hold their eggs and raise their young. There's a feeling of life and energy, and it's the perfect time to start heading out after school to look for some free dinner-time supplements!

DANDELION

One of our most abundant and well-known 'weeds', dandelions are an ideal healthy food that we can enjoy collecting in that short time period after school. Dandelion leaves – and roots – can be eaten at any time they're growing, but they're at their absolute best in spring, when the new, fresh leaves begin to sprout. Compared with lettuce, they contain significantly greater quantities of vitamins A and C, protein, fat, iron, phosphorus, calcium and carbohydrate. They create a natural super-salad that can be eaten on its own or ideally added to another salad as a supplement.

What you need

+ Collection bag (a sandwich bag or similar)
+ Plant-identification book/app

What to do

1. Keep your eyes peeled for dandelion leaves. Many plants can frequently be found growing together; if so, there's likely to be an abundance.
2. Once identified correctly, pick the leaves and place in the collection bag ready to take home.
3. When you're collecting the leaves it's really important to guide the collection process. As it's a low-growing plant it's important

not to pick any leaves from the side of the road or in areas where people and dogs regularly walk. Dandelions do tend to grow in obscure and sometimes seemingly unhealthy places, such as along the edge of a busy road, but there are always plenty in more remote and suitable locations. It's a matter of common sense and choosing leaves from clean environments.

4. Always wash the leaves thoroughly in cold water before eating them.

BIRCH WATER

I discovered birch water as a youngster. I soon became fascinated by the process of collecting it and the mechanisms involved in the tree that enables such a product to be harvested. It's an incredible process, so simple and interesting to witness. This doesn't work at all times of the year, so it's important to be ready to make a collection of birch water in the spring when the tree fluids are flowing at their peak. The process is called 'tapping', and there are specific devices made for this, but it can be done really simply in a couple of easy steps.

What you need

+ A drill with small drill bit
+ A small twig
+ An empty 1-litre bottle/container
+ Duct tape or bungee cord

What to do

1. Find a birch tree. These are common trees and should be at least 25cm in diameter at chest height. Anything less and it's likely the process won't work.
2. Always seek permission from the owner of the tree before collecting the water or sap.
3. At around 1 metre from the ground, drill a very small, slightly upward-directed hole a few centimetres into the tree.
4. Stick a small twig into the hole (a matchstick will do, depending on the size of hole you've made). It shouldn't plug the hole, but loosely fit inside.
5. The fluid should begin to drain out of the hole and run along the stick.
6. Use the duct tape or bungee cord to tie the bottle around the tree so that its opening is just below the stick coming from your hole.
7. Ensure the fluid is dripping from the stick and collecting in the bottle.
8. Once the collection method is secure, you can leave it alone for an hour – or, ideally, all night.
9. The time of year will make a difference to the speed and quantity of flow. At their greatest flow levels, the quantities can be absolutely incredible and a litre can be collected in an hour.
10. It's really important to seal up the hole afterwards so the tree doesn't continue to leak its precious fluid. Press the wooden plug right into the hole you made so the seal is tight and stems the flow of liquid.
11. The best way to seal the hole is to use candle wax, which can be melted and pressed into the area to fill any extra gaps. This should stop the fluid, sap will form and the tiny injury to the tree will disappear in no time.

Gathering birch water is a fascinating process. But the best bit comes when you take your first sip of the cool, fresh liquid together with your children.

SUMMER

Finding food in summer is partly a continuation of the foraging that takes place in spring. Spring gives the freshest, smallest, sweetest natural foods, and in summer many of these ripen during the warmer months. With longer days, time outside can be stretched before bedtime and activities can be kept going for longer.

CHANTERELLE MUSHROOMS

We tend to go a little further afield in the summer after school so we can head off in search of chanterelles, a common wild mushroom. These little orange, fruity mushrooms are absolutely delicious.

What you need

+ A collection bag (sandwich bag/small basket)
+ A plant-identification book/app
+ Fire-starting materials (see 'Light a fire', page 120) or a portable camping stove
+ A small frying pan
+ A small knob of butter, or splash of olive oil
+ A clove of garlic, sliced

What to do

1. Chanterelles can be found in mixed (deciduous and coniferous) and pure coniferous woodlands. Their orange colouring and wavy shape make them stand out from other species of mushroom that may be around.
2. If you do come across a mushroom that looks like a chanterelle, use your identification book or search online to make a positive identification. This is vitally important. If you have any doubt, leave what you've found behind.
3. Carefully pick the positively identified chanterelles, taking only what you'll need.
4. Light a fire or your portable camping stove and cook them on the spot, or take them home to cook. They are best fried in a pan with a little bit of butter or olive oil and some sliced garlic. Even a child who turns their nose up at mushrooms usually won't be able to resist the delicious-looking and -smelling food presented before them.
5. To repeat: please make sure you know for certain that the mushrooms you've picked are chanterelles. Eating mushrooms that you're not 100 per cent sure about is extremely dangerous, so check, check and check again.

Mushrooms, by Jasper. None of these is edible, beware!

AUTUMN

BLACKBERRY COLLECTING

Blackberries – the fruit of the bramble plant – grow on most
hedgerows, footpaths and field edges. The bramble is a really
common weed that spreads like crazy every year and takes over if it's
not cut back. But it produces the most amazing fruits.

What you need

+ A collection bag (sandwich bag or similar)
+ A pair of gloves (optional)

What to do

1. Blackberries are at their best from August to October, depending
   on the year. If the fruits are not yet ripe, go back in a few weeks
   or when you judge they'll be ready. Some years give a better
   harvest than others, but if you go looking at the right time you'll
   find at least some.
2. Take care when picking blackberries as the spines on the plants
   can scratch your hands. Wear gloves if you prefer, but these do
   interfere with the process of collecting – soft blackberries are
   easily squashed – and you might be better off without them!
3. Don't pick the berries that are growing too close to busy roads
   or to the ground, especially in areas where dog walkers are
   common – for obvious reasons.

Filling a bag with blackberries – and returning with purple-stained fingers and lips – is the sign of a good hour out in the countryside. Most of the time we don't actually come back with anything because it's all been devoured on the way home, but if you have restraint it can be a cracking natural, healthy, free dessert packed with vitamins, collected after school!

> *One of my youngest son Jesse's first words was 'blackberry'. Our garden hedge is thick with blackberries in early autumn, and every day he'd make me stop, lift him up and help him to pick them. Stuffing them into his mouth and smearing the purple juice into his newly washed clothes. It was always a battle to pull him away from that hedge, but I didn't mind – they're delicious and healthy, nothing but goodness for the growing lad!*

WINTER

The trees are bare, the berries are gone, and everything's a little bit cold and bleak. If my children are anything to go by, your child will probably be coming home cold and grumpy after a day at school. Having spent all day inside because it's too wet to go out at lunchtime or breaktime, this is the perfect opportunity for them to get a little bit of fresh air. So take that step and make the effort to go out for a little while.

Winter is a brilliant time to try out some outdoor-cooking methods. There's nothing better than a campfire in the cold winter air – you really feel the benefit of the fire and it makes everything even more satisfying.

OUTDOOR COOKING

What you need

+ Fire-starting materials (see 'Light a fire', page 120)
+ Tin foil
+ Sweet potatoes and a selection of other vegetables (e.g. sweetcorn, peppers, courgettes, carrots)
+ A small quantity of olive oil, and a few garden herbs
+ A plastic sheet/picnic rug to sit on
+ Warm clothes

What to do

Sweet potatoes

1. Light a fire somewhere in the garden: in a fire pit, in a hole dug out of the lawn, in a flower bed, wherever you can.
2. Allow the fire to burn fiercely for a while, then let it burn down so that a good pile of hot embers remains smouldering away at the bottom.
3. Take a roll of tin foil and choose something to cook. It's difficult if not impossible to find food out and about in the winter, so you'll have to cheat a little, but this can still be fun.
4. Wrap some sweet potatoes – cut in half if they're on the big side – in two layers of foil.
5. Throw the foil-wrapped potatoes in among the hot, glowing embers, banking the embers up over them and taking care not to rip the foil. Sweet potatoes cook in no time at all in the embers of a fire. It's so simple, but the act of preparing the fire for cooking, wrapping a potato in a couple of layers of foil and literally throwing your dinner into the fire is so much fun.

6. Under strict supervision, allow your child to move the potatoes gently around in the embers with a stick, again taking care not to rip the foil, to ensure that every side gets thoroughly cooked.

7. Once the potato feels soft and squidgy all around it'll be ready to throw on a plate or, even better, be carefully eaten right there in their hands.

8. It's not only sweet potatoes that cook well in this method. Sweetcorn, peppers, courgettes, indeed any vegetables can easily be cooked in foil parcels in the embers of a fire.

Other vegetables

1. Take a mix of vegetables on a chopping board outside.

2. Allow your child to roughly cut up all the vegetables with their penknife (see 'Use a penknife', page 35).

3. Create a tin-foil bag with sealed edges.

4. Throw the vegetables into the bag with a drizzle of olive oil and perhaps some garden herbs, if you have them. Then place them carefully in among the embers of the fire, turning the bag occasionally. Pull the bag out from time to time (watch you don't burn your fingers), open and check whether the vegetables are ready.

5. Make sure you throw the same kind and size of vegetables in the same packages. The last thing you want is a mix of cooked and uncooked food.

The benefit here is that your child is cooking their own dinner. It's also encouraging them to try vegetables because they'll be far more willing to eat something they've cooked themselves.

Challenge

The idea with this is that it's kept simple, to start with at least. As
you do this more often – perhaps it even becomes a regular thing
you do together – you can get more adventurous with the types of
food you're cooking and the flavours you produce. I hope to get to
the stage where once a week we're eating great-tasting, healthy food
outdoors, whatever the weather, cooked by the kids. Something to
work towards, at least!

SUNRISE MOMENTS AND SUNSET CHATS

OK, so one of these will have to be done before school, but, please, if
you don't do anything else in this book, promise me you'll do this ...

What you need

+   An alarm clock

What to do

1. Set the alarm to go off before dawn on a morning when you know
   there will be a clear blue sky.
2. Get up while it's still dark.
3. Have breakfast ready for you and your child – something quick
   and easy. Take it with you or have it at home before you leave.
4. Head outside and find an elevated spot. This could be the top of
   a high-rise building with an open and clear view of the sunrise

or it could be a hill in the countryside. An opening in a hedge overlooking the horizon will do as well. It really doesn't matter, as long as you can see the sun as it comes up.

5. Make sure you're at your location before the sun breaks the horizon and sit. Simply sit and watch, together.

6. Watch the sun in the distance rise up, filling the sky in front of you with light and colour. Watch it steadily climb and change every few seconds as the day breaks and warmth spreads over your world. If you're lucky your child will have sat there and watched, noticeably appreciating what they are seeing in front of them.

It's likely your child will be like my children, more interested in running about, digging holes, climbing a tree or moaning about being cold. That's fine too – don't get frustrated, it's all part of it. Our children are not adults. They don't appreciate things in the way we do and they understand them differently. That doesn't mean they don't notice and, more importantly, it doesn't mean you shouldn't do these things.

I'm not pushing my children into doing anything. I'm not making them play rugby, go to dance class, learn an instrument or climb a tree. But I am giving them opportunities to do all of these things and more, like watch the sun rising. I'm giving them the chance to stay up a little later one evening after school and sit on the bonnet of our car at the edge of a field and watch the sunset, opening up appreciation and interest in life, and, more importantly, doing so together.

When I was younger I was that child who was more interested in other things. I wanted to get moving, play something, find something, build something, run around and move on to the next thing. I wouldn't show any interest in the sunrise but it didn't mean that I didn't feel it. I know children do when they are exposed to it because I did. Now I'm a little older (albeit not much wiser), I appreciate these moments because I was shown them when I was young.

We learn as we get older that our parents were sometimes right and that perhaps we all turn into them to some degree, for better or worse. My mum and dad were consistent with the opportunities they gave to me to try things and see for myself. Now I'm a little older and see the benefits, I want to give that to my kids.

I believe it's the same in many other aspects of life. Take sport, for example. How have any of our champions on the field of play risen to those heights? Well, everyone went through their own battles on their own individual paths, but everyone has something in common. At some point they were given the chance to try their sport for the first time. Opportunity is everything. I was given the opportunity to take up rowing at the age of 16 by a school friend who had been down to the local rowing club on a weekend starter course. I had no intention of trying rowing before that – I knew nothing about the sport. But my mate said to me, 'Alex, try it, you'll love it.'

For many weeks I resisted, but, eventually, just to shut him up I relented and went down to Evesham Rowing Club. Because of that opportunity, my life changed for ever. I went on to pursue a career in a sport I loved. After a long and winding road in pursuit of excellence I walked away with two Olympic gold medals. At the root of those two gold medals was the initial opportunity.

WATCH WILDLIFE AFTER DARK

I've always loved wildlife. In fact I think it's been the most constant thing in my life from as far back as I can remember. It's a deep fascination, but I'm still very much an enthusiastic amateur. Wherever I am in the world – and whoever I'm with – I'm always pointing things out or looking for wildlife, whether in cities, towns, countryside, mountains or beaches. Wherever we are, and whatever time of day or night it is, I'll have my eyes peeled and I'll be listening out.

What you need

+   All your senses!
+   A torch/headtorch

A one-winged owl, by Jasper. I'm told the owl is posing best-wing forward.

What to do

1. Once it's dark, wrap up warmly and take a walk outside.
2. Being out in the dark really gives you the chance to wake up your senses and it provides a great opportunity to change the emphasis from one sense to another. For example, in the daytime the sense of sight is generally most important for wildlife-spotting. At night the sense of sound is more important.
3. Set the challenge to walk as quietly as you can with your child. You'll hear rustling, movements, creaks and cracks as animals move off into the distance.
4. Listen out for owls, such as the sharp screech of a barn owl or the call of a female tawny owl.
5. Listen for the haunting bark of a dog fox or the incredibly loud call of a male deer.
6. There are so many different sounds unique to the animals that make them. If you walk quietly with your senses alert, you'll build up a fantastic picture of what's around you without even being able to see anything.
7. Try to remember what you've heard. Record the sounds, if you can, and identify them later. There are huge resources for nocturnal animal calls online.

Movements and sounds generally don't pass me by when I'm outdoors. It's nothing hard – there's definitely no skill involved – it's a natural habit that's developed over the years. I owe it to my dad, who was always pointing things out, stopping, taking a deep breath and watching. My grandad wouldn't ever go on a walk anywhere without his binoculars, and whether it was birds, buildings, boats, hills or people, he was always looking at something in the distance, interested in what was going on out there in our environment.

I've started to see this tendency developing in my children. Jasper, Daisy and now even young Jesse point out the red kites circling overhead in the morning or the deer high on the hill in the distance. Noticing things gives us an interest in and an appreciation for what is around us. With appreciation we start to care, and when we care, we do something about it and look after it. We need to encourage our kids to look after the natural world, because before long they're going to be the ones in charge.

BAT HUNTING

For those interested in wildlife, a really fun activity as the sun is setting is going out bat hunting. In no way am I suggesting you run around the woods with a net in the air trying to swat these aerobatic artists out of the sky. Far from it. I'm suggesting an activity infinitely more sedate, but one that does require a small financial investment.

What you need

+   A bat detector (easily purchased online)

What to do

1. Head outdoors just before dusk.
2. Turn on the bat detector and listen out for the clicks the machine makes.

A very happy bat, by Jasper. We didn't see this, just to be clear.
Pure imagination!

3. Test out different locations if you don't hear anything the first
   time. Bats, sadly, aren't found everywhere, but it shouldn't be
   long before you find some.
4. A good place to start searching for bats is around water, which is
   the habitat of many of the small insects on which they feed.
5. As you listen to the sounds the bats make, talk about what
   they're doing. The more you listen, the more of a picture you'll
   be able to build up. You'll start to understand the patterns in
   which they fly around and the sounds they make while hunting
   for their prey.

*Recently, Jasper, Daisy and I joined a group for a dusk walk with a bat
expert, who turned up with a collection of bat detectors. Each of us was
armed with one of these relatively inexpensive beeping machines, and
we walked across fields and down dark wooded tracks hoping to pick
up the high-frequency clicking from some of the local creatures.*

*It didn't take long. The clicking started moments after turning
the detectors on, indicating a bat flying overhead. Looking up and*

scanning the sky, you could hear the bats way before you could ever spot them flashing past. The sounds really built up a picture in our minds as to where the bats were and how many of them were flying around. Most fascinating of all, you could track them hunting for dinner. As the bat flies, it uses echo location to bounce sound off passing insects. When it closes in on its tiny prey – a mosquito, for example – the sound increases in pitch and frequency right up to the point of contact. You can't see all this happening but with these detectors you know exactly how the hunt is going. It's a brilliant activity for kids: exciting, interactive and great for getting the imagination working. After this experience we bought a detector online, and we now always chuck it in the bag when we head out for a night in the outdoors.

As the winter months close in, the bats will also start heading indoors to begin their annual hibernation. This obviously means the bat detectors will be useless until spring, when the bats appear again.

STARGAZING

On a clear night, an absolute must-do is to lie on your back and stare up into the night sky. Turn off torches, house lights and car lights, and put your heads close together and stare into the darkness. As your eyes adjust you'll start to see more and more stars in the blackness above. This is always best in areas furthest away from artificial light, such as up a mountain or deep in the countryside. It's incredible how much light a city sends up into the atmosphere, but that doesn't make urban stargazing impossible. Even in the heart of cities stars can be visible, perhaps not to the extent of in the wilderness, but there can still be some really great views. The best bet in a city is to try to get high up above the lights, so a rooftop or balcony would be ideal, if access is safe and easy.

What you need

+ A rug or mat to lie on (yoga mat or picnic rug)

What to do

1. Spread the mat or rug down on the ground somewhere that's furthest away from any lights.
2. Lie on your back, look up into the sky and observe.

SHOOTING STARS

+ If you stay in one place for long enough – and if you're really lucky – one of you may spot a shooting star. It's the most exhilarating yet frustrating thing because it's gone before you really appreciate what you're seeing.
+ Shooting stars are small pieces of rock or dust moving so fast that when they hit the Earth's atmosphere they heat up and burn, causing the flash of light in the sky.
+ Occasionally the piece of rock is large enough not to burn up completely and does in fact hit the ground. This is what we know as a meteorite.
+ To find a meteorite must be up there as one of life's dreams. Keep your eyes peeled if you haven't found one already!

INTERNATIONAL SPACE STATION (ISS)

+ My favourite night-time sighting is something far more consistent. The International Space Station (or ISS) orbits the Earth continuously.

+ Check online or look at one of many apps that tells you exactly when the ISS will be flying overhead. There are hundreds of other satellites orbiting the Earth and it's easy to mistake these for the ISS, so do check to find out the correct time and direction of travel for your location.

+ If there is no cloud cover and you've a clear view of the sky, you'll most likely see it!

+ This orbiting spacecraft is, among other things, a science lab in space. Since the year 2000 astronauts have lived on board the ISS and have been conducting scientific research ever since.

+ The ISS completes its orbit around Earth every 90 minutes. Depending on where you are on Earth and where it's flying, you can spot it more than once in an evening.

+ At some angles it looks huge, bright and so incredibly obvious. At other times it's much more faint.

+ Lying back, watching this spacecraft 400 miles up and imagining the people on board is something truly amazing – a fascinating thing and difficult to comprehend.

Challenge

Every Christmas Eve when it's a clear night we make sure to head outside a few minutes before the ISS is due. We'll wait for it and watch as the satellite flies overhead, and we'll tell the kids that it's Santa delivering presents somewhere else in the world before coming to us later that night. It's a sure way to bring even more magic to the evening.

PLANETS

+ It's possible to see Mercury, Venus, Mars, Jupiter and Saturn when you know where to look in the night sky. Use a telescope or binoculars to look at these planets.
+ When you identify Jupiter, look out for its moons. There are four, which can be viewed through binoculars or a telescope – it's an extraordinary thing to see!
+ You'll need a steady hand to look through binoculars and spot these moons.
+ Use a tripod or create a makeshift tripod by lying on the ground and stabilising your binoculars on something solid, such as a table, rock, fence or tree stump.

CONSTELLATIONS

+ There are some fantastic apps that you can use together and which mirror the night sky as you hold the phone up and move it to where you're looking. This incredible technology connects the sky it's seeing with its data and tells you exactly what you're looking at. Knowing the names and locations of the constellations – the word given to recognisable patterns of stars, such as Orion, the Plough and Cassiopeia – is something I really wish I was better at, but with these apps you can learn to recognise them with ease.

It's funny how ideas and interests can change into trends. Through discussions during the long hours on rowing camps while waiting to go training or racing we'd develop interests together. For a few years the Great Britain men's rowing team had a real interest in the night sky and as a group we became big stargazers. We'd often head outside after dark and look up into the sky to try to spot constellations, planets, satellites and, of course, the ISS. One of the guys once pointed out the direction of another galaxy. We didn't believe him at the time, but after some further research and gazing at length through binoculars and a telescope we realised he was right, and that we were looking at the Andromeda galaxy 2.5 million light years away!

We were so lucky to have the opportunity to go to some wonderful, remote places around the world. A regular training camp was at a place called Aviz in Portugal. About three hours' drive from Lisbon, the hotel there is an architectural masterpiece in the middle of the countryside, run by two wonderful friends, Luis and Pedro. The structure of the building meant you could walk up on to the wooden roof easily from the ground. At night we'd lie on our backs, chatting and watching the sky, seeing everything there is to see and a whole load we didn't know about. We used apps to recognise constellations and check when the ISS was flying overhead. Those were wonderful times on warm nights in a big group of mates.

30-MINUTE ACTIVITIES

'A journey of a thousand miles must begin with a single step.'

Lao Tzu

There are times in all of our lives when we just need to spend a day indoors: maybe we're fighting an illness or feeling low; we've just had a busy week with some late nights or the work is piling up and we simply have to get it done. Or perhaps the weather is terrible and we can't bring ourselves to go outside.

Life with kids is incredibly hectic, and we often struggle to keep it together, be organised and get to all the places we need to get to. Sometimes it feels like time is slipping away without us even realising it and we haven't done half the things we're supposed to do. That's why these activities are ideal. You can always squeeze a 30-minute period outdoors into your day, no matter how busy you are. It's always easier to do if you have a reason to be doing it. I'm hoping this section will motivate you to go outside; provide the seeds of inspiration to help you take that first step. And just because it's a short period of time, that doesn't mean it's not going to be memorable, interesting or fun.

Quick inspiration

+ Go on a stepping-stone walk
+ Dig a hole
+ Identify an insect
+ Watch cloud creatures
+ Make a bow and arrow

FINDING NORTH

There's so much technology around now that knowing how to navigate 'manually' isn't really necessary, but it's interesting and fun, and you never know – one day it could be the difference between life and death. It's also a good way to start conversations around directions, the Poles, magnetism and maps, and is certainly a challenging skill to grasp.

USING A WATCH

You can use an analogue watch face and the sun to accurately show which direction north is. This method relies on you knowing where the sun is in the sky, so it doesn't work on an overcast day, but it's an incredibly useful method of navigation in the right circumstances.

What you need

+ An analogue watch
+ A sunny day

What to do

1. If you're in the Northern hemisphere, hold the watch horizontal to the ground and line up the hour hand with the sun.
2. Halfway between the hour hand and the 12.00 marker on your watch will be the direction of south. You can then use that to check your direction of travel and to find north.
3. If you're in the Southern hemisphere, the method is subtly different.
4. Point the 12.00 mark on your watch towards the sun.
5. Halfway between that mark and the hour hand will be north.

Once you know north or south it's simple to find the other directions, so you'll always know where you're going. This method only works if your watch is operational and the time is correct. If it's not, you could be heading in any old direction.

MAKE YOUR OWN COMPASS

A great activity while you're on the go is to make your own compass. Whether it matters or not in which direction you're going, it can be great fun finding out by using this quick and easy makeshift method. It's a really practical exercise that your child will love learning and trying out with you.

What you need

+ A magnet
+ A needle
+ A flat leaf
+ Water

What to do

1. Take the magnet and rub it over the needle continuously in the same direction about 15 to 20 times
2. Place the flat leaf on the surface of the water. This water could be in a puddle in the road, in a birdbath or a cup. It doesn't matter as long as the leaf can fit on the surface and float freely, and the water is perfectly still.
3. Now carefully drop the needle on to the leaf and watch what happens.
4. The magnetised needle will spin to align with the Earth's magnetism. One end will point north and the other end will point south.
5. You won't necessarily know which end will be which at this point, but using other methods in this book, and remembering that the sun rises in the east and sets in the west, you should be able to work it out. When out for a walk with your child, they can try to figure which is which, and you can test them as a challenge.

NAVIGATIONAL METHODS

What you need

+ Your eyes!

What to do

Trees and moss

1. If you're out in the countryside it's sometimes possible to tell north by looking at the trees.
2. In some cases moss will grow on the north side of a tree in the Northern hemisphere. The north side of a tree is generally more shaded and doesn't receive the sun during the middle of the day, which causes the vegetation to dry out on those sides that are in the sun. Mosses like moisture, so they'll prefer to grow on the damper – northern – side of the tree.
3. This is, however, not a hard-and-fast rule. It's a great thing to notice and observe, but there are other reasons why moss could be growing on sides of a tree that aren't pointing north.
4. If the tree is being shaded on one side by another tree, foliage, a bank or a wall, these conditions will provide the moisture that's good for moss growth, even if it's on the south side of a tree.
5. Some tree bark holds moisture better, too – a deeply crinkled bark, for example, may create a cooler, wetter environment suitable for moss growth, independent of the direction it's facing.
6. Using moss to navigate is a useful tool to have, but as your sole navigational aid it could be risky!

Wind

1. Another useful indication of the compass points is the prevailing-wind direction of a particular region.
2. The UK, for example, has a prevailing-wind direction from the south-west.
3. Because trees are more often being pushed towards the north-east due to this wind, they'll begin to grow in that direction. This means that trees are more likely to be leaning away from the south-west and pointing towards the north-east.
4. If you go to an exposed hilltop, for example, the hawthorn trees that you're likely to see will all be pointing towards the north-east. Test this out for yourself.
5. The problem with this principle is that trees and plants grow towards the light by a process called phototropism. In the Northern hemisphere, with the most light throughout the day coming from the south, trees do often grow towards the south, which counteracts the influence.
6. Trees do provide other directional clues, however. On the northern side, branches tend to grow more vertically than horizontally, and on trees or plants that grow berries, the quantities tend to be greater on the southern side.

Stars

1. Head out for a walk at night.
2. You can still direct yourself without any modern technology if you use the stars.
3. Try to find the group of stars known as The Plough, which looks like a deep saucepan (see diagram, page 83).
4. Trace a straight line from the edge of the saucepan furthest away from the handle.

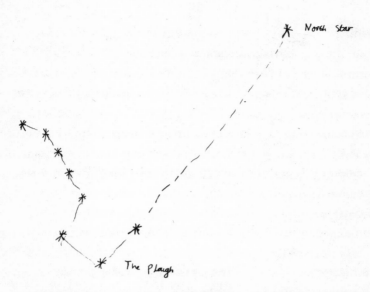

The Plough, by Jasper. Every time we're out at night it's the first thing he spots.

5. The bright star around five times the distance between the two stars of the saucepan edge will be the North Star, sometimes known as Polaris.

6. The Plough rotates around the North Star – in fact, all of the stars in the sky do – so sometimes it will look as though the North Star is above The Plough, and at other times below.

7. The distance between the saucepan edge and the North Star will always remain the same, however, and the North Star will always be situated above the North Pole. So if you travel in the direction of the North Star you'll always be going north.

8. This method, of course, relies on there being a clear night sky. Under cloud, when the stars aren't visible or when they're hidden by buildings or trees, navigating this way is somewhat tricky. Maybe this would be the right time to make your own compass.

Finding your direction and navigating by these natural methods needs thought and consideration. It can be a really interesting exercise and mental puzzle. Sometimes it's clear and obvious; at other times it takes numerous pieces of the jigsaw to be put in place before a decision can be made. A little lateral thinking and you can make some good observations to distinguish whether you're on the right track. Every time I'm out on foot or in the car with Jasper, who now really grasps these concepts, I test him and ask in which direction we're heading. In our family I'm – annoyingly – renowned for getting lost and not having much natural feeling for direction. Unfortunately for me it's true so I've learnt these fun little tricks and methods over the years to help me and at least make me think about it more. Nowadays, Jasper usually gets the direction correct more often than I do. But I'm OK with that.

Challenge

One 30-minute activity we sometimes try to do is to head outside and walk in a certain direction for half the time, then turn back – 15 minutes north and back, for example. It's creating a reason to get out, and it's a bit of an adventure as it changes the concept of a normal walk. Normally, going on a walk means we're going somewhere, to a point or to a place. But now we're simply going in a direction. It involves intrigue and interest, and to keep on track you'll need to think. Unless you're in the middle of nowhere, you'll have to navigate around places – houses, fields, objects, private land, rivers and ponds – just to keep going in the same direction. It's rare that you'll be able to choose a direction – north, south, east or west – and simply walk in a straight line. Keeping on course while navigating a route is a great challenge!

While rowing across the Arctic Ocean we were reliant almost completely on the electronic navigation equipment that was installed on the boat. The GPS would tell us in which direction to go, our speed, longitude, latitude, distance travelled and distance to go, and we even had an autohelm on board, which, once a grid reference or waypoint was typed in, would steer us automatically to that exact point. We became reliant on this equipment.

Problems arose for us, however, when we began to lose power on board. Our batteries were running low and, due to the bad weather, the autohelm device was having to work overtime to keep us on the course we'd set. Big waves and rough seas were knocking us off course and so our power usage was extensive. Unfortunately, our solar panels weren't charging the batteries up as much as we needed as a result of the miserable cloud cover (mainly nimbostratus). We soon became desperately low on power and were forced to turn off our navigation system.

Fortunately, we had a magnetic compass on board. Using this, our skipper selflessly sealed himself into the cabin, safe and dry for 48 hours, and steered us rowers towards the tiny Jan Mayen island. We rowed like crazy through the rough, unpredictable and dangerously cold sea to make it safely to what turned into our final destination. And what if we hadn't had that magnetic compass? Well, navigating to a tiny spot of land in a vast grey ocean would have been next to impossible!

TRACK ANIMALS

Some people still rely on tracking animals when they go hunting, wildlife watching or researching. The skills these men and women possess, which have been passed down from generation to generation, are incredible. The sense that these hunters have is otherworldly to us in our modern Western society, where the only tracking we do is to find our mobile phones when they get lost or to locate our parcels when they are being delivered.

Tracking animals properly takes years to master, picking up skills through trial and error, and practising them outside day after day. My children and I often go out animal tracking, but because of our lack of skills and tracking knowledge we have to do it in a much more basic way. OK, we don't end up with dinner at the end of it, but we do have great fun discovering which animals are out there and working out how they move and where they go. I must admit that it's not easy, especially in the places we go. Footpaths enable you to cross the countryside, but of course they're riddled with human and dog prints mixed up among the wild-animal tracks you're trying to see. If you're lucky enough to find some unspoilt areas with good animal prints in the ground, then make the most of that and learn as much as you can.

What you need

+   Eyes!

What to do

1. Head out for a walk and try to find some outdoor areas that are less well trodden by people.
2. Ensure you have permission to be on the land.
3. Move slowly and encourage your child to look at everything.
4. Check out the ground, hedges, fences and trees.
5. Keep your eyes peeled for animal footprints in the mud or any other signs that wildlife has been around. It would be very unlikely for you to find no evidence of animal activity at all.
6. Examples of wildlife evidence: fur caught in fences, holes dug in the soil, trees and branches chewed, droppings and footprints.

Challenge

Over a period of time build up a map that you add to each time you go out animal tracking. You won't necessarily always see something new, but when you do you can put what evidence you've spotted on to your map. Over time you'll see where the rabbits feed, the birds roost, the badgers walk and the deer graze. It may be that you never actually see these animals, but you'll know they are there.

I was taken on a really interesting afternoon out around a nature reserve a few years ago by an ecologist. She was an expert in every plant, animal and insect we encountered, and I loved it. I knew very few of the species, so it was fascinating. We were in a part of the country with large expanses of water – lakes, rivers, streams and ponds – so river-living creatures were high on our agenda. We set out looking for otters in a particular area because apparently they were common and regularly seen slinking off into the water. Well, of course on the day

Common animal tracks

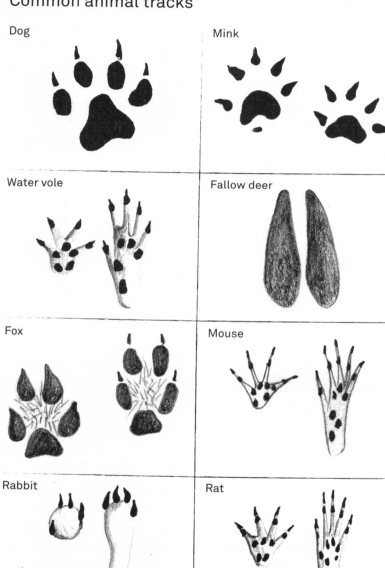

Dog

Mink

Water vole

Fallow deer

Fox

Mouse

Rabbit

Rat

Squirrel

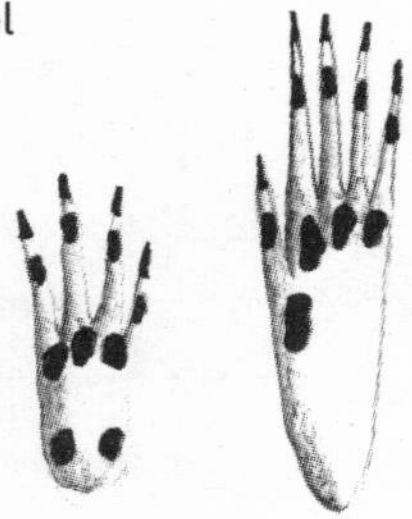

Otter

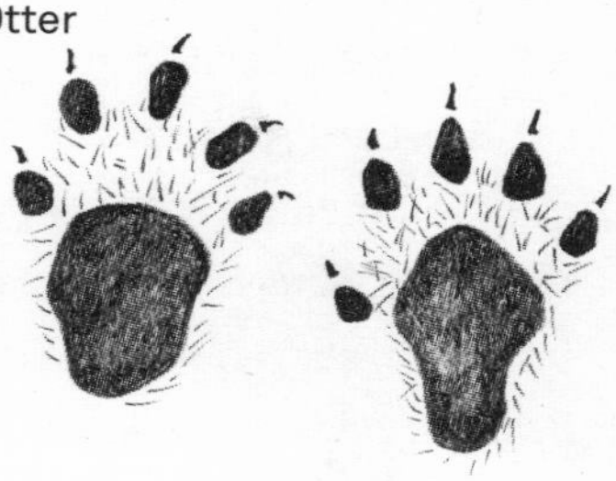

Hedgehog

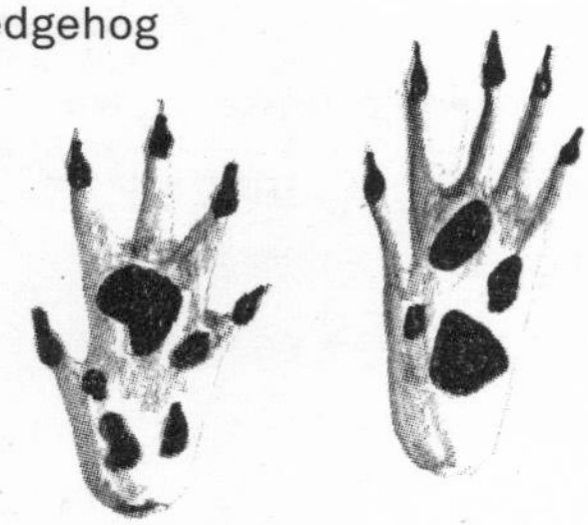

Mallard

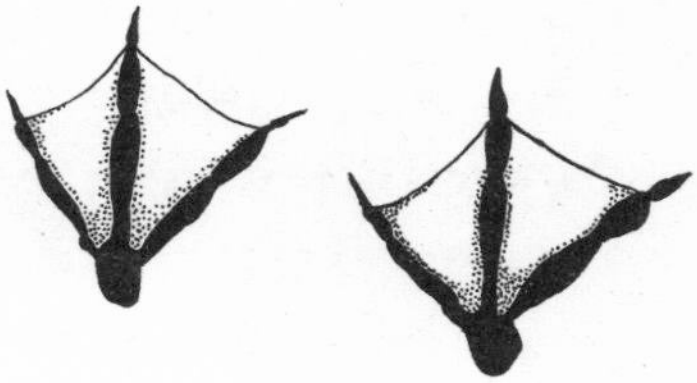

Muntjac deer

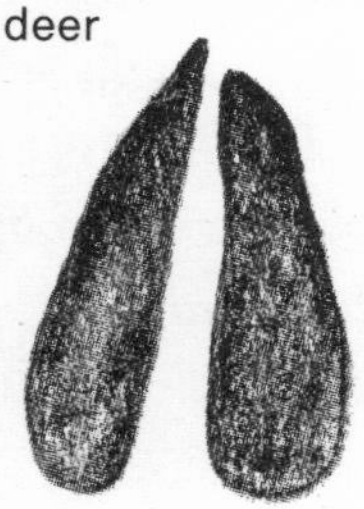

Carrion crow

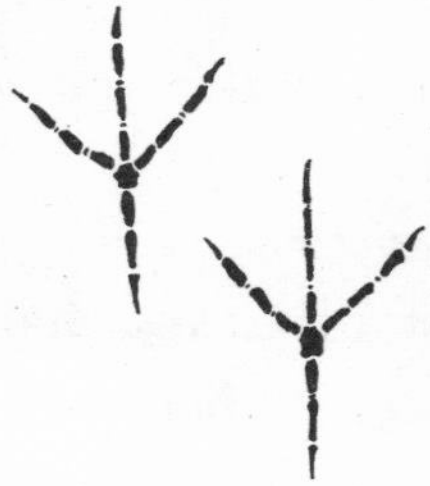

Badger

T. rex

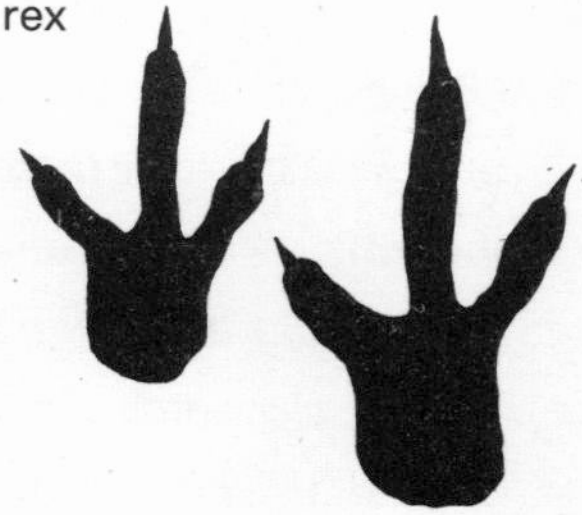

I was there they were nowhere to be seen. There were no footprints, droppings or evidence of feeding – nothing. Slightly frustrated, we walked back to habitation ready to call it a day.

As we crossed a small stone bridge among a group of houses, Phoebe, my guide, suggested we just have a quick look underneath the bridge. Sometimes, just sometimes, otters enjoy the shelter that bridges provide. It was on my hands and knees, in the dusty, dry dirt next to a small trickling, clear stream crunched up under this bridge that I came across the first bit of wild-otter evidence I had ever seen – otter poo. Phoebe spotted it first. Now it sounds disgusting and not very interesting, I know, but this was such an exciting find for a number of reasons. First, it was definite proof that otters were in fact in this area. Otters are great indicators of healthy water systems, so it was fantastic to see evidence of them in the wild here. Second, we were alongside human habitations, next to houses, under a bridge! Searching in the wilds earlier, where humans rarely visit, we'd seen nothing. It was right on our doorstep that we found the droppings! Finally, most surprisingly, the thing about all of this was when Phoebe picked up the otter poo in her hand, brought it up to eye level and took a long sniff. Not only did it shimmer as the fish scales embedded in it reflected the light, but it smelt sweet and really nice! I was shocked by how surprisingly pleasant the smell was.

Now, every time we walk along a riverbank or near a bridge I make sure we always look for evidence of otters. Months later I took my kids along to look under the very same bridge. Unsurprisingly, there was fresh evidence there, this time with very clear footprints (it was obviously a well-used and popular otter spot). I urged Jasper and Daisy to pick it up and take a sniff, which they both did eagerly, and like me they were pleasantly surprised by the smell. I'm so pleased I could teach my kids this little-known fact about otters – that their poo smells *great. It's a tiny little thing, but it's interesting and unusual, and I'm sure they won't forget it.*

A path in the woods may seem the same every time you walk there, but once you start really looking and taking notice, a whole new world opens up. As soon as you see the footprint of a rabbit you can start getting into the mind of that rabbit. Begin a discussion about where it's going and what it's eating. You'll see a rabbit hole with droppings, then a chewed-up branch a little further along, some grass that's kept short in one patch and a bit of fur that's got caught in the fence as it's crawled underneath. You'll soon begin to build up a picture of where it's going and what it's doing.

Starting off with the more common animals that are everywhere, you'll quickly begin to distinguish the difference in the signs and evidence they leave behind. It's a great place to start, and, gradually, as your eyes adjust and become more aware, you'll start sensing things before you actually see them. I realise it's a strange thing to say, but see for yourself. Hopefully, and I'm sure it will be the case, if you encourage this with your child, they'll quickly overtake you in the observation stakes. They'll be taking you out and teaching you all these things.

DISCOVER BIRD-OF-PREY PELLETS

Not everyone knows that birds of prey or raptors produce something called a pellet. It enables the birds to 'vomit' up a pellet-shaped piece of indigestible material they've eaten. Depending on the species of raptor, these pellets come in slightly different shapes and comprise different waste material. Owls, for example, will produce pellets made up of rodent fur and bones, while kestrels are more likely to have many more beetle shells and casings in their pellets. Of course, the 'ingredients' in these pellets will depend on the habitat and the time of year when these birds are hunting.

What you need

+ Collection bag/sandwich bag
+ Wildlife-identification book/app/website
+ Gloves

What to do

1. If you're lucky enough to know where a bird of prey roosts, then head straight there. If not, keep your eyes peeled and look carefully.
2. Encourage your child to look under branches, below perches or ledges in any isolated building (as long as it's safe to do so and you have permission), or under any structures you come across.
3. Collect as many pellets as you can find.
4. Dissect the pellets to discover what's inside. To some adults this may seem disgusting – I get that, I really do – but to a child it's something amazing.
5. Pellets usually take the shape of a dropping, because they have to come up out of the bird's throat, but they aren't waste in the same way that droppings are.
6. Depending on which bird the pellet is from, you'll see different things inside based on their diet.
7. Your child can break open the pellet and discover the last few meals of the bird in question. There will probably be bones – the best is always tiny little skulls. Often these mouse or shrew

skulls are whole and in good shape; sometimes, if you're lucky, you can piece together whole skeletons.

8. Owl pellets are fantastic, as their diets are relatively straightforward. They consume some of the larger species of rodent with relatively bigger and more robust bones. These often remain whole and easily identifiable.

Once you know where a roosting site is, you'll have a constant supply of these pellets, as long as the birds aren't overly disturbed. If your child is anything like me or any of my children, you'll very quickly start to build up a bit of a bone collection, which is a fascinating hobby, if not a little weird. Like many things, once you start to see these natural phenomena you'll notice them more and more. Once you know they're there, and have an interest in them, you'll become ever more knowledgeable and curious.

Birds of prey are highly sensitive to human intervention. Their food sources are very susceptible to interference from humans and

A kestrel, by Daisy. Not dissimilar to her humans!

because these birds are high up the food chain, a small change lower down can lead to big problems higher up where they exist. Doing something simple, like building a nesting box in your garden or local area, could make a significant difference to the population of birds of prey in your area.

Moving house as a youngster was one of the most exciting things we did. We moved from a tiny cottage in our village to a large old farmhouse in the middle of a field just a stone's throw away. I remember a great deal about the dilapidated, derelict shell of a house we'd soon be living in. There were mouse skeletons on the steps in the cellar and hundreds of dead pigeons in the chimneys. It was the discovery of a roosting kestrel in the barn that really excited me, though.

I spent one afternoon climbing the beams of the old open-fronted Dutch barn at the back of the house. The wind would whistle through gaps in the sheets of rusty black corrugated iron that formed a semi-weatherproof shell around some ancient piles of hay. In its prime, this would have been a grand hay barn. Now, it was my adventure playground. Shimmying along, 15 feet off the ground, hands blackened with rust and a hundred years of dust and grime, I felt a wing whistle past me.

Turning quickly around and nearly losing my grip, I just spotted the tail feathers of a kestrel as it disappeared at pace across the fields. I'd obviously startled it as it flew in for an afternoon rest in the quiet, dry barn. Not expecting to see me up there in the rafters, it had turned quickly and fled. As my shock subsided, I realised I was now among a pile of bird pellets. I knew exactly what they were, and now, having just had that close encounter, I knew exactly which bird they'd come from. Feeling my way along the beam I stuffed my pockets with as many of the pellets as I could find, then made my way down. Jumping the last six feet or so, I scoured the ground beneath me to see if there were any more. To my delight, there was an enormous amount. It was clear that this must have been the kestrel's favourite and regular roosting site. I felt sad for disturbing it, but excited that I could investigate these pellets.

I took handfuls of them home and spent a happy few hours separating the tiny bones from the undigested fluff and shiny beetle casings. It was amazing to see how many tiny mammals and insects the kestrel must have consumed, and to be given the opportunity to build up a picture of this wild animal's diet. Around 20 years later, the memories remain as clear as day.

Picking open the pellet of a bird of prey is a memorable thing to do outdoors. Just remember not to transfer any fears or revulsion that you might have to your children. If it's safe, interesting and educational, then encourage it. This activity is exactly that, even if it might not be your preferred activity on an afternoon out!

CONSTRUCT A SOLITARY-BEE HOUSE

There are thousands of bee species in the world, the majority of which are known as solitary bees, meaning they don't live in colonies like the more well-known honey bees or bumble bees. You're quite likely to come across a solitary bee when you're out in the park or roaming the countryside. These bees will dig out a hole in a suitable piece of ground where they'll lay an egg, seal off the chamber and repeat the process close by. If the ground is ideal for them you may find hundreds of bees all in the same area, digging holes, making it look like a colony – but they'll all be solitary bees nesting together!

We always feel like we've struck gold when we find a nest spot because it's as if a tiny little documentary is screening right there in front of our eyes.

What you need

+ Cow-parsley stems (bamboo poles work well too)
+ A plastic bottle
+ A sharp knife
+ A fine-toothed saw
+ A piece of string (see 'Make string', page 31)

What to do

1. Collect a good few handfuls of cow-parsley stems in the late autumn/early winter, once these tall straight-standing plants have turned white and are easily broken.
2. Cow parsley grows up like crazy from the ground in the spring and summer months, is always found in hedgerows and can often tower over an adult by the time the growing season is over. When growing it has green, moist stems, but once the growing season stops it dries out, and turns white and brittle.
3. Cow parsley is easy to identify and harvest but easily broken, so be careful when handling it.
4. Carefully cut your stems into 20cm lengths.
5. Bees won't access the hollow cow-parsley stalks if the edges at either end are too rough and splintered, so make sure the cut is clean.
6. Cut the top off the plastic bottle, leaving a wide opening.
7. Push the cut stems into the bottle, filling the space so they are compacted inside, tight and unmoving.

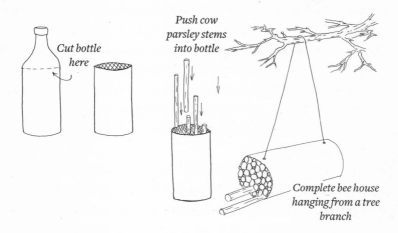

Cut bottle here

Push cow parsley stems into bottle

Complete bee house hanging from a tree branch

8. If you've used bamboo just do exactly the same, but be aware that bamboo grows in blocked sections. Ensure there is an entrance for the bees!

9. The beauty using of cow parsley is that its diameter changes as you move up the long stem, cutting off pieces, giving the bees a range of tunnel sizes.

10. Make sure you use even the really thin stems, as you'll create tunnel options for a whole range of different bee species. It's estimated there are some 20,000 bee species in the world. In the UK there are around 270 bee species, 250 of which are solitary. These range greatly in size, so by providing different-sized nesting tunnels you'll have more chance of success.

11. The bottle will provide a weatherproof covering for the tunnels, and you can hang it somewhere in the garden, on a porch or in a tree.

12. Hang the bottle in a south-facing position. Bees are cold-blooded and rely on the warmth of the sun in the mornings. Use your outdoor navigation skills to identify the correct

direction before you position the bee house (see 'Finding north', page 78).

13. Bees are most likely to take residence in your solitary-bee house if the tunnel entrances are clean, smooth, dry and clear of any foliage or debris. They may sound fussy creatures, but if they haven't dug and created the site for themselves they'll only use a suitable substitute site.

Play around with the types of tubing you use and the positions in which you place the nests in the garden. See what species end up living in the tunnels. If there are solitary bees in them you'll see that the entrances are blocked up with mud, meaning they've laid an egg inside. Do note that spiders often use these as dry areas in which to live. By doing this you're helping create a safe environment for the wildlife in your local area and again you're raising your children's awareness about what's out there. When they see an animal living in something they've made, they'll be pleased and take a keen interest in it in the future.

Challenge

How about a cow-parsley-stem sword fight? Challenge your child to a fight with these stem swords – the first to break the other's sword completely is the winner. They are long but snap easily on connection so are very safe. The games are sometimes short, though!

BUILD A TINY KITE

I was shown how to build incredible little kites by my travelling Australian relatives. On their way around the world, they'd sell their home-made kites on the streets of towns and cities and at festivals, and make a great deal of money. I was fascinated by the mini contraptions, but the most amazing thing to me was how well they'd fly, how high you could get them and the fact that you didn't need much wind for them to take to the air.

Daisy flying a tiny kite, by Daisy. I've never heard her laugh and cry so much at once!

What you need

+   Stems of straw, reeds or strong grass
+   Coloured tissue paper
+   Glue
+   Scissors
+   A cotton reel (the longer the better)

What to do

1. Collect a handful of straw, thin dry reed or strong long grass from whatever source you can find – riverbanks, gardens and fields. At a pinch, florists can provide something similar for this purpose. The material must be light and rigid – the lighter the better.

2. Cut a piece of straw 15cm in length and another piece 10cm in length.

3. Cut a piece of tissue paper in a 'kite' shape 15cm from top to bottom, 10cm at its widest point.

4. Very carefully and sparingly glue the pieces of straw to the paper, the longest piece first and the shorter piece across the middle at the widest point.

5. Cut two thin strands of paper 50cm long, 1.2cm wide.

6. Carefully stick these two long tails to the bottom point of the kite.

7. Tie one end of the cotton reel to the centre point where the two strands of straw cross. There may be a small gap that the thread can be pushed behind to tie on to the kite. Make sure this is secure.

8. Allow the glue to dry. Once dry, it's time to set the kite into the air.

9. Choose a dry day when there's a gentle and steady breeze. If the breeze is too weak, the kite won't lift off; too strong and the kite will rip apart.

10. The tails are important to stabilise the kite, so experiment with their length. Too long and the kite will be weighted down and won't fly well; too short and the kite will fly uncontrollably, spin and sink to the ground. Better to start with a longer tail that can be easily cut.

11. A gentle flutter and movement from side to side is ideal.

12. As the kite is only attached by a single thread, you won't have control over its flight. With a long cotton reel you can really get some height on these kites.

Jasper flying a kite, by Jasper. It was a brilliant little kite until it became stuck in a tree.

13. Use a rock, fence post, tree branch or a shoe to weigh the end of the line to the ground and simply leave the kite dancing up there in the sky.

Challenge

These kites are so quick, easy and cheap to make you could spend 30 minutes one day making a number of them. The next time the weather is ideal you could take them all out and set them all flying together, tying them up along a fence or something similar. Why not have a go at adapting the design of the kites to see which one works best. It's extremely satisfying seeing your little creation right up there against the clouds, and if you tie them off it enables you to share a moment together as you lie on your backs in the grass looking up at your kites flying around on wind power alone.

I have very happy memories of flying these little kites out in the garden. They're completely safe and will cause no damage if they fall or crash. If they blow away they'll very quickly decompose and cause no harm to the environment. Using nature to provide entertainment is important – here you're utilising a breeze to create a moment. You can start talking about how to use air currents and your child's imagination can be stimulated with stories of flying creatures and explorers.

COLLECT RAINWATER

Have you ever thought about drinking water that hasn't come out of the tap from a filtered, chlorinated chemically enhanced source? Have you ever drunk from a beautifully clear, cool mountain stream or dreamed of finding a natural spring bubbling up out of the ground and drinking that delicious fresh water? Well then, why haven't you collected and drunk rainwater?

One of the things I was most eager to tell my mates about when I'd return from a family camping trip as a youngster was that we'd drunk water from a stream. I don't know what it is, but there's something magical about it – the simplicity of it, the way it really does take you back to basics. Without going as far as hunting, gutting and skinning an animal, it's as basic as you can get. It made me feel tough, even a little bit hardcore and dangerous.

What you need

+ A plastic sheet (e.g. a shower curtain)
+ Four sticks, each around 1 metre long. Garden canes are perfect.
+ Some string
+ A clean bowl/tin can/water bottle/bucket
+ Rain

What to do

1. Spread the plastic sheet on the ground in a suitable location, somewhere that won't get disturbed and with a clear view of the sky above.
2. Start at one corner and press one stick into the ground, ensuring it is at an angle and firmly embedded.
3. Lift one corner of the plastic sheet and tie it in a knot around the top of the stick, or use some string to tie the corner of the sheet onto the stick.
4. Repeat with each corner until the plastic sheet is held up off the ground.
5. There should be a sag in the middle and the sheet should not be touching the ground.

6. If you have trouble keeping the sheet off the ground and the wooden stakes firm, use string tension to hold the poles in place by tying it to the top and securing the other end to the ground. This will take some juggling and patience, but it is a great challenge to work out together.
7. Pierce a hole right in the centre of the plastic sheet with a pen or a pencil. A small hole will do, certainly no bigger than 5mm across.
8. Place the bowl or water container directly underneath the hole ... and wait.

Hopefully you've set this up when it's raining, so water will start to be collected immediately. The amount you collect will be completely dependent on the size of your sheet of plastic and the intensity of the rainfall, but even if you only manage a couple of sips of water each, it will be the best-tasting water you've ever drunk.

I love this simple activity you can easily do in 30 minutes. It's something constructive, healthy and fun to do together outdoors when it's raining, and teaches your child that water doesn't just come from the tap – the natural world does indeed provide. When you start introducing water to the conversation there are hours and hours of discussions to be had about where it comes from – and where it goes!

Challenge

If you manage to collect enough water, why not pour your collected water into a bottle and – if you're camping, like I was – take it home with you. The water can then be transferred into ice-cube trays and on the following day you can all be having rainwater ice cubes together around the dinner table. Personally I prefer them in an evening G&T, but I wouldn't recommend this for the kids.

Back in the days of summer holidays at my grandparents' farm I used to take the black, fire-worn kettle over to the rickety old wooden bridge that crossed the stream and dip it over the side. One of the jobs for us kids when we arrived was to dig the water-collection spot deeper so the kettle could be thrust right down into the fast-flowing water without disturbing the sediment. The kettle would fill right up to the brim, then I'd haul it back to the fire, latch it on to the hanging hook over the flames and wait for it to start bubbling away.

After a few minutes over the heat of the fire the water would be boiling. We'd leave it for a couple of minutes, water spilling from underneath the lid and fizzing in the flames below as it instantly evaporated. Thoroughly boiled (three minutes at least) we'd then carefully pour the water over the tea bags – leaves, grit, sticks and all – leaving it to stew. The water was always slightly brown or yellow, but every cuppa was delicious and no one ever got ill in all the years we visited. Well, I did once, actually, but that was because I ate too many sweets – nothing to do with the water!

I was proud of using the resources we had available to us and living a basic lifestyle, as we were doing. I'd return to school with an enormous sense of pride and satisfaction, feeling brave and daring, like an explorer who'd returned from the wilderness. I was pleased to learn something new every time we went there to stay – what to eat, how to find things, build things and burn things. We never collected rainwater, though ...

BREW COUNTRYSIDE TEAS

OK, so this isn't for everyone, but I do recommend that everyone tries it at least once in their lives! It's an incredibly simple way of getting back to nature and feeling like a real-life outdoors person – or even one of our distant hunter–gatherer ancestors.

There's an enormous amount of information about the identification of plants, and it's worth getting an ID guide to take with you on your countryside tea-hunting trips. There are now also apps available that will help to identify what you're looking for. It's really important to make the correct identification when you're planning to consume a plant. These recipes couldn't be more simple and they're not only fun to follow but also seriously healthy.

What you need

+ A plant-ID book/app
+ A collection bag/basket

What to do

1. Head outside and keep a watchful eye out for the plants you're looking for. There are plenty of options outdoors for teas and wild foods, but I've come up with some really common, easily identifiable and quick-to-do recipes.

STINGING-NETTLE TEA

Stinging nettles can be found almost everywhere, but they prefer to grow in nutrient-rich, fertile soils that have been disturbed, which aerates the roots. Nettles thrive on building sites and vegetable gardens for this very reason. They start pushing through the soil in early springtime, and if you can catch them then they're at their very best. Nettles will grow well into autumn, although the larger, older plants aren't so appealing.

What you need

+ A pair of gloves
+ A mug
+ A pan to boil water in over a fire, or
+ A camping stove and a pan, or
+ A flask of boiling water

What to do

1. Head out in search of a big patch of stinging nettles.
2. This activity is best done between March and August, when nettles are readily available and growing well.
3. Try to avoid patches of nettles that are close to roads or along footpaths where human and dog traffic is high and where there could be any human airborne contamination. The last thing you want is contaminated leaves.
4. With your protective gloves on, pick the very top shoots and small nettle leaves. A couple of handfuls will do – you don't actually need that many, but smaller, fresher leaves are better than big old ones.

5. Put the leaves and shoots into your mug, tearing them up as you go.

6. Pour over the boiling water that you've either heated on a fire or on your camping stove, or that you've brought with you in a flask.

7. With a stick – or, if you're really organised, a spoon – stir up the tea, releasing all the goodness and flavour.

8. After a couple of minutes fish out as many of the leaves as you can and you'll be left with steaming green water – nettle tea!

9. You don't have to take out all the leaves. In fact, some people eat nettles in a similar way to wilted spinach. Once they've been left in boiling water for a while, the sting disappears and they're a really healthy, delicious addition to a meal. Nettle leaves can even be a fantastic side dish with curry.

I must admit it's not always the most delicious tea – I certainly enjoy the process of making it more than the actual drinking – but nettle tea is really healthy. It's full of vitamin C and a good alternative to water. Collecting the nettles is a great challenge and teaches children the importance of taking care while being brave at the same time. It's great fun and a fantastically simple activity to do together, but it can certainly end in tears if you're not careful!

What strikes me about kids, however, is that once they've overcome a fear or completed a challenge, rarely does it stand in their way again. My daughter, Daisy, was terrified of touching stinging nettles and refused point-blank to do it. After some persuasion over many weeks she picked a leaf with her bare hands without getting stung, and the smile on her face was enormous. She hated the taste of the tea – but you can't win them all!

With great intentions we took off outside to make nettle tea one cold, grey half-term afternoon. The kids were crawling up the walls after being cooped up indoors for too long. I'd had some work I had to get done and they'd spent the morning waiting with ever-decreasing patience. I found myself agitated and irritated as I hadn't finished what I was supposed to have done and didn't feel as though I could afford the time out. Filling my bag with a few essential items, however, we set off at a pace across the fields.

After a short distance we were all starting to feel a bit better. My stress was being exhaled from me and I was starting to see clearly again in the fresh air, while Jasper and Daisy were running off their pent-up energy. Settling down at the edge of a hedge, a huge supply of new young nettles to my side, I handed out the gloves and the kids started collecting leaves. Most of the time with gloves on you're pretty safe, as the tiny stinging hairs on nettles don't penetrate, but this was not one of those times. Daisy was badly stung when she walked straight into a bunch of nettles held by Jasper. All hell broke loose, tears flowed and screams rang out across the countryside.

Undeterred, but with Daisy inconsolable, we pushed on, lit the small camping stove, managed to boil up some water and threw in the tear-drenched nettles. While we left the leaves to steep in water we managed to find some dock leaves for Daisy's stings, and she gradually began to calm down. Peace was eventually restored and it was time to test out our nettle tea. As I picked up the metal pan we'd been boiling the water in, the base of the stove to which it was still attached caught on my boot. Slipping out of my hands, the stove toppled over on to the grass, releasing all of our precious hard-fought nettle tea.

We all sat in absolute silence. Waiting for my reaction, the kids were still as statues, then all of our eyes met over the next few seconds and we burst out into laughter. What a disaster. We all agreed it would probably have tasted horrible anyway and Daisy admitted she'd never liked nettle tea. Traipsing our way back home, not long after leaving in the first place, we were all laughing even though we'd had a nightmare. We'd been outside for not much more than half an hour and in that short time a lot had happened in our little world. We were refreshed, excess energy had been spent, we had laughed and cried – and were all ready to get back home!

ROSEHIP TEA

An alternative to nettle tea is rosehip tea. It's an August to November tea-making activity, when the big rosehip seed pods are bright red. Rosehips can be found in hedgerows all over the place, and wild rose bushes are often laden down with the seed pods. You can very quickly get a good haul, but do be careful when you collect them, as rose thorns are extremely sharp.

What you need

+ Rosehips
+ A pair of gloves
+ A mug
+ A pan to boil water in over a fire, or
+ A camping stove and a pan, or
+ A flask of boiling water

What to do

1. Be sure to wear thick gloves when you're collecting the rosehips.
2. You don't need that many hips – five to six per cup should be adequate.

3. Once you've collected all the rosehips you need, find a suitable place to cut them open.

4. Using a knife, slice them in half long ways. Inside you'll find a whole load of yellowish seeds that are covered in tiny hairs. Be careful here because the hairs are really irritating if they get into your skin. Rosehip seeds were the original itching powder, and a handful of these hairy seeds thrown down someone's shirt is a pretty nasty trick! The hairs work their way into the skin and can end up being really painful. In light of this, it's really important to remove all of these seeds and hairs because in the mouth and throat they can be extremely unpleasant.

5. Once all of the seeds are removed and discarded, you should be left with beautiful, clean fleshy red shells. Cut these up into pieces and chuck them into a mug. This whole process is a bit fiddly, so if you can get a few people on the job at once, many hands make light work! It's totally worth the effort when you're done, though.

6. Mash up the cleaned-out rosehip flesh as much as you can in the bottom of the mug to break them up and release the flavour.

7. Pour over the boiling water that you've either made on a fire or on your camping stove, or that you've brought with you in a flask, and mix it around for a few minutes. After a while the water will change to an orange-pinky colour. Don't bother trying to get out the pieces, but if there are any tiny hairs floating on the surface then scoop them out. You can strain the fluid to remove the pieces and ensure there are no hairs remaining using a piece of cloth, pair of tights or even a sock. I've used my sock before and the kids loved it. They thought it was absolutely hilarious. I'm not suggesting it makes the best-tasting tea or is the most hygienic, but it's good fun and an ideal way to separate the rosehips from the tea.

8. My preference, however, is to eat the dregs afterwards. They're delicious, full of vitamin C, and the kids will love the taste as well as getting the chance to eat something they've picked and processed.

Top tip

Use rosehips later in the year once they've been outside in a frost, as the fruit becomes softer and sweeter after the plant cells have been broken through freezing. For this reason, if you ever collect rosehips to use at any other time of year and are not going to use them straight away, then always take them home and freeze them.

There are plenty of other rosehip recipes, such as jams, sauces and jellies. Rosehips really do taste amazing, with a delicately sweet, floral fruity taste. The hips are good to use right into December – the older fruits become sweet and sticky as the months progress, and can be mushed up and spread on bread to make a deliciously sweet, wild-foraged jam.

HAWTHORN-LEAF TEA

Hawthorn leaves are easy to find in most hedgerows around the countryside, and hawthorns also grow as small trees in and around fields. Quite often they're found standing alone right at the top of a hill, shaped by grazing animals and the wind. When I come across such solitary trees I'm reminded of big bonsai trees. They have incredibly sharp thorns on their branches, which is why they're so useful for hedges and keeping livestock in fields. Hawthorn is easily identified in the autumn, when their branches are covered in small bright-red berries, which are also edible, but it's in spring when the tea is at its best!

What you need

+   Hawthorn leaves
+   A mug
+   A pan to boil water in over a fire, or
+   A camping stove and a pan, or
+   A flask of boiling water

What to do

1. Choose young fresh leaves (these can also be added to salads) and put them in the bottom of your mug.
2. Pour over boiling water.
3. Leave for a couple of minutes to steep, in which time the water will change colour slightly. You'll be left with a subtle nutty flavour – really delicious!
4. Either remove the leaves or keep them and eat afterwards.

With all of these tea recipes it's not necessarily the final product that's the important thing. Yes, in each case it's a healthy, free drink, but it's the process that's really crucial here. As with everything in this book, it's about having a reason to get outside; about the process of going in search of something, finding it, processing it into a product that you can consume together. There are no rules. These ideas are just seeds to get you started, to get you out and about.

Challenge

There are so many possibilities for foraged plants and foods that you can gather outdoors for free. Here's a delicious addition to an outdoor meal, one that's incredibly easy to make.

ROSEHIP SAUCE

Roseships have been used for centuries, originally for their reported medicinal effect and now mainly for their delicious taste. With a little bit of effort you can make a delicious little accompaniment to your picnic or outdoor snack when you're out and about in the countryside. It can turn a family walk into much more of an adventure, while adding in a little relaxation to the day out.

What you need

+ Rosehips
+ A knife
+ A pair of gloves
+ A metal cup/bowl
+ Teaspoon of honey
+ Camping stove or fire-lighting equipment (optional, see 'Cook over a fire', page 140)
+ Water

What to do

1. Pick a few handfuls of rosehips.
2. On a plate, chopping board or tree stump, wearing gloves cut open the rosehips and clear out all the yellow seeds and hairs. This can be a fiddly job and, depending on the ripeness of the hips, can get quite sticky, so you'll ideally have some water to hand to wash your fingers afterwards. Do your very best to remove as many of the hairs as possible.
3. Place the de-seeded rosehips in a metal cup or bowl and mash them all together with a spoon or stick.

4. Cover with a small amount of water to keep the rosehips moist
   and increase their volume.
5. Place over the fire or stove and bring to the boil.
6. Allow the mixture to heat up, stirring every now and then to
   prevent any burning or sticking to the metal container.
7. Add a teaspoon of honey to the mixture to sweeten.
8. Once the mixture reaches the consistency of watery golden
   syrup, take it off the heat and enjoy!

This is a wonderfully quick and delicious addition to an outdoors
picnic or snack in the countryside. It's great on bread, oatcakes,
biscuits – just about anything. Your child will love the taste and will
have really enjoyed making something over fire with you!

TWO-HOUR MISSIONS

'A man who dares to waste one
hour of time has not discovered
the value of life.'

Charles Darwin,
The Life and Letters of Charles Darwin

Getting outside is sometimes easier when there's a particular
purpose to the outing. Of course, there doesn't always have to
be, but having an objective can turn a rainy Sunday disaster into a
productive, memorable experience. There's so much to look at, do
and find outdoors – and you don't even have to go very far to do it.
Right outside the front door, down the street, in your garden or local
park, there's an adventure to be had. So decide where you're going
and what you're going to do, and be on your way!

We all have busy lives, but sometimes we manage to find or
make some significant time to pursue longer, more time-consuming
missions. The ideas here are designed to be just that, projects that are
more engrossing, with the potential to teach your child useful skills.

Quick inspiration

+   Play hide and seek
+   Take a rain shower
+   Swim in a river
+   Make a swing
+   Take-a-photograph walk

LIGHT A FIRE

Please note: To light a fire in a public area, be it forest, heathland, field, park or any outdoor area, you must first get permission from either the landowner or forest service. Some areas are designated safe zones for fires and barbecues, but otherwise please do seek permission.

What is it about fire that so fascinates us? Fire is ingrained in the human psyche – it's part of our history, helping our ancestors long ago to survive and become the dominant species on Earth. Fire defined civilisations, enabling the processing of food and the development and manufacture of tools and weapons. It was also used for warmth, safety, protection and power. Fire is incredibly powerful and even dangerous, but if used correctly it's also so much fun.

I believe that introducing children to fire is important because everyone must learn to respect it, and that it's your job as an adult to share an understanding of this energy that changed humanity for ever. Whether it's to warm you up on a cold evening in the garden or to cook over on a longer adventure, the use of fire is a skill that should be mastered and utilised. There's nothing better than sitting around a campfire cooking, roasting marshmallows, or just staring into the flames chatting. From kids to adults, we can all appreciate fire, but there are a few things to know first.

I've spent many, many hours desperately trying to light a fire using only friction between two pieces of wood. After just ending up with a pair of blistered, bloody hands, I discovered that the wood I was using was the wrong type or that I wasn't doing it fast enough in the right direction. Thankfully now, after years of practice, I can pretty much light a fire under most conditions, but you do need a little bit of knowledge to be able to do this. It's an incredibly difficult process when you're starting out, with a number of factors that have to be exactly right in order for it to work. It's great fun learning these skills, however, and it's a fantastic thing to try to do together as a family. When you eventually start to see smoke, your first flame pops up and you feel the heat against your fingers, the sense of satisfaction and achievement is extraordinary. I don't care who you are – your first fire lit by friction will never be forgotten.

There's always a temptation to make fires too big. It can be great fun, but always think of the risks. A bigger fire is likely to be hotter and more prone to spread out of control. Keep fires small and manageable, especially when children are around. I always think about how quickly I could put it out in a hurry if I needed to, and whether there is a large-enough water supply to do so. What's more, the bigger the fire, the more fuel you'll use, and if it's down to just you finding and hauling the wood around you may be more content rationing it and keeping the size down.

Before lighting a fire, it's really important to be prepared. Once started, time is of the essence, and if you don't have what you need to hand it could mean the difference between success and failure.

What you need

+ Tinder
+ Kindling
+ Fuel
+ A spark

TINDER

Tinder is any sort of dry material that will catch alight on contact with a spark or flame. It could be cotton wool, tissue, dry grass, lichen, tree bark, fluff off a jumper or wood shavings. Whatever it is, it should be dry, so if you intend to get a fire going on a day out think about this and think about how to keep it dry. I love the stories of survival experts who collect tinder as they walk, stuffing wet material under their clothes so that their body heat dries it out in time for their campfire later. I'm not suggesting you go that far ... but it's something to think about.

There are a great number of different natural tinders that you can gather when out and about. If you know what to look for – and know how to process them – each one is a fantastic way of getting a fire started.

Birch bark is a superb tinder that you can use even in wet conditions. It's easy to identify birch trees – their bark is usually silver in colour and papery in texture, and they often have black diamond shapes and 'eyes' on their trunks. The thin bark is easy to peel off the trunk without damaging the tree, and to start a fire you only need a small quantity.

Either peel the bark into thin strips (the thinner the better), or scrape away at the bark with a knife to create a fine bark powder. If you're doing this, find a sheltered spot. There's nothing worse than creating a beautiful pile of fine tinder powder, only to see it blown away in a gust of wind ... or by a child's sneeze. Birch bark contains highly flammable oils that light easily and make the whole fire-lighting process that little bit simpler. Preparing the tinder is a delicate process and great for getting kids really engrossed in what they are doing.

Western red cedar bark is another great tinder. These trees are easily identifiable by their spongy soft, feathery red bark and their

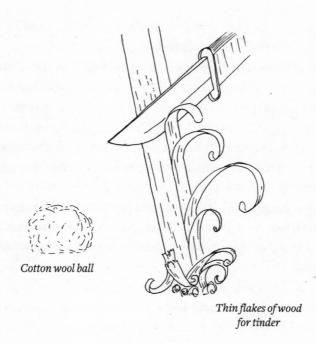

Cotton wool ball

*Thin flakes of wood
for tinder*

fronds of evergreen foliage that smell of pear drops or pineapple. They're worth seeking out if you really want to make fire-starting easy! The bark can easily be scraped or picked off the tree without causing damage, and you can collect a very suitable little bundle in no time at all.

Top tips

I'm all about making the fire-lighting process as easy as possible. Although I love the challenge of creating a friction fire and being as pure as possible when lighting it, the reality is that it's extremely difficult, especially if you live in a country where rain is a common occurrence. In some cases, pure is great; otherwise, especially with children who have wavering patience levels, you just need to get it going! So, when you know you're intending to head out and light a fire, take some tinder back-ups with you.

One of the very best tinders is *cotton wool and Vaseline*! Cotton wool is a fantastic tinder in itself, but it does burn fairly quickly. If you add Vaseline (petroleum jelly) – or even lip balm – to the cotton wool, you'll get a much longer-lasting flame that will burn slightly hotter, which will improve your chances of getting your fire going. Dip your cotton-wool ball into the Vaseline to get a thin covering, then break up the ball, mixing the Vaseline into the fibres as much as possible. You're looking to create a very loose ball with fine fibres that will easily catch a spark. The Vaseline is highly flammable due to its oil content, making a perfect fire lighter even on wet days.

Candle wax is brilliant for chucking into your tinder pile. It won't take a spark, but once a flame is lit it will melt into the tinder and keep the flame going for longer. This will give you more time for the next stage of the fire-building process and increase the chances of the fire being a success. Keep a few old candles, tea lights or just pieces of candle wax in your outdoor-coat pocket just in case.

KINDLING

Once the tinder has lit it will burn very quickly. The whole point of tinder is to turn a tiny initial spark or ember into a flame that will allow other dry material to catch alight. Fires all start small and need to be built slowly and gradually to increase heat. Adding kindling is just the next stage of this process. This dry material could be wood chips, more dry grass, dry leaves, twigs or small sticks. It's usually a good bet to find wood that contains plenty of sap – pine twigs, for example. These take to burning really quickly and easily, and are great for getting a fire going.

Pine trees often have branches still attached to the trunk that have died as the tree grows. This is not an indication of an unhealthy tree, it's simply the way these trees develop – as they grow taller, the branches underneath the green canopy die off. This creates an amazing resource for kindling. If you find yourself in coniferous woodland you'll easily be able to gather the materials to start a fire within seconds of creating a flame using these dead dry branches as kindling. You'll only need a small handful to really get the fire going; it will soon become burning hot, which will allow you to build your fire into a sustainable heating and cooking tool. Using these branches as kindling is a foolproof method, even in wet weather.

Generally, the thinner and drier the wood, the better for nurturing a fire into life. With a knife you can shave off strips of dry dead wood and gradually grade up the sizes of the kindling you're using.

FUEL

This is what will keep the fire burning when the heat has really developed. Once the kindling has taken and produced a good heat, larger logs and branches can be introduced into the fire. At this stage even damp material will burn, although it's always better if it's dry. Collecting fuel can be a great challenge as you conduct races to see who can make the biggest pile, who can bring the longest branch and who can find the driest wood. Turning these jobs into a game makes the whole experience so much more fun and satisfying when you're all sitting round the end product together. These games don't always work, I have to admit. Sometimes kids just expect instant results, in which case I might just change the plan or stick with it and attempt to teach them patience.

In an ideal world you'll build up little piles of tinder, kindling and fuel next to where you want your fire, giving the process the greatest chance of working. A good gradient of sizes from kindling upwards is really useful, so you can add the smaller, thinner pieces first and gradually add the larger pieces as the heat of the fire grows. In reality, this rarely happens with kids! Kids want to play, they want to have fun – and so they should. To them, grading wood is as pointless as tidying their bedrooms, so don't worry about it. As long as you have some pieces ready for each stage, you'll make it work. And, remember, more tinder and kindling are always better than less.

SPARK

Once all the materials above have been collected and prepared, the spark is the final piece of the jigsaw. There are so many different ways to generate the spark, and some methods are much easier than others. I always make sure I keep a box of matches or a lighter with me on a day out just in case we can't get the fire going any other way. It's always a fun challenge to light the fire without using a match or lighter, however, so do your best to keep them in your pocket.

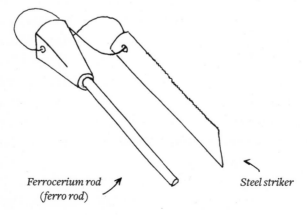

Ferrocerium rod ↗
(ferro rod)   Steel striker

FERROCERIUM ROD (FERRO ROD)

A ferrocerium rod is very basically a strip of metal along which you run a piece of steel at speed. This will produce a shower of sparks that will catch alight when directed on to your tinder. It's a really fun and exciting way to get a fire going, and as long as your tinder is suitable, you'll be sure to get it lit and create that much needed flame. There's a bit of technique involved to improve the chances of success, but – very simply – create the sparks close enough to the tinder and you're off!

When you buy a ferro rod in an outdoor shop or online, most of them come with a 'striker'. This is just a piece of steel that's harder metal than the ferro rod, although the back edge of your penknife will work just as well, if not better. Because it's a dynamic movement, with a spectacular sparking result, kids love to do it. I have to stop my kids sending sparks into the air just for fun and using up all the ferro rod, but I suppose that's all part of the game and they're relatively inexpensive. Readily available in the right places online, these are a must-have for exciting outdoor-fire-lighting experiences. Combine a ferro rod with the cotton wool and Vaseline tinder, and you have a matchless fire-lighting trick in absolutely any weather.

What you need

+ A ferro rod
+ Some tinder
+ A good supply of kindling and fuel

What to do

1. Hold the ferro rod just above a pile of suitable tinder.
2. Hold the striker or back of a knife blade firmly against the ferro rod.
3. With firm pressure push down swiftly in a scraping motion to create a flurry of sparks directed towards the tinder pile.
4. Repeat this firm pushing motion until the tinder has taken a spark and burst into flame.
5. Very carefully, add kindling to the flame, the smaller and drier the better to start with as the fire builds its heat.

BATTERY AND FOIL FIRE

It's great fun to imagine being marooned on a desert island with just a few items at your disposal. The challenge is to start a fire to cook your food using only what you've found on the beach or what's in your pocket. You can set up this scenario and really challenge your child to do this with you. All of the fire-lighting methods just described could be employed, but this is a slightly more unusual one, using things you can find at home.

What you need

+   A strip of tin foil
+   A penknife/scissors
+   A cotton bud
+   Lip balm/Vaseline
+   1 AA battery
+   A good supply of tinder, kindling and fuel

What to do

1. Cut the foil into a strip 1cm wide and 7cm long.
2. Fold the strip in half so the two 1cm-wide ends meet, and make another cut from one corner right to the other corner, creating two triangular pieces.
3. There should now be two pieces, one with a straight end and another with an extremely sharp point.
4. Remove the cotton wool from the cotton bud and cover lightly in lip balm.
5. Fluff up the cotton wool into a ball as much as you can. It's amazing how much cotton wool is actually on a cotton bud ...
6. Very carefully take one piece of foil and hold the flat end on the positive (+) end of the battery.
7. Take the second piece of foil and place on the negative (-) end of the battery, ensuring the foil pieces do not touch each other.
8. With your free hand, bend the foil so the two pointed ends are very near each other, able to touch with a little gentle movement of the fingers.
9. Hold this pincer-like foil above the cotton ball, bringing it down towards it. As you touch the two foil ends together, you'll see a spark form, and, if the cotton wool is in close proximity, it will take the spark, catch alight and burst into flames. When this happens it's instant and quick! Be prepared. The lip balm or Vaseline in the cotton wool will help it burn for a little longer, giving you more time to gently add your dry tinder and kindling material.
10. You've just started a fire using a battery! It's a great trick. It takes a bit of skill, and the kids will need help to adjust the positions of the foil, but you're sure to get a result.

11. Be warned, though, as you can end up burning your fingers if you're not careful. The pointed ends of the foil need to be really thin and fine, otherwise the current will just flow through the foil, generating heat in the metal part of the battery on which your finger is placed. The lighting moment will be quick and brief.

Top tip

If you have chewing gum to hand, use the paper – foil gum wrap, which is even better than foil for this method of fire lighting. The foil will take the current from the battery in the same way, but because there is paper attached, that will catch alight too. As long as the points of the foil are really thin, the spark will form and the flames will arrive.

FRICTION FIRE

Creating a fire through friction is the ultimate challenge and provides the greatest satisfaction when successful. If ever there's a high-five moment in life, it will be when you achieve this together, a moment that you and your child will never ever forget. Once you manage this, you'll feel like you can take on the world!

What you need

+ Some strong string or cord to create a bow
+ A flexible piece of wood, 50cm long and 1cm in diameter, to create a bow. Hazel is ideal.
+ A dry, flat piece of wood to use as a base plate
+ A penknife/saw

+ A 30cm-long piece of dry circular wood, as straight
  as possible
+ A flat piece of wood as big as your palm

What to do

1. Tie some strong string or cord to each end of the 50cm piece of
   wood, creating a bow. The pole should be bent slightly in a curve
   and the cord pulled taut, creating the bow.
2. Along one edge of the dry, flat piece of wood, cut a small 'V'
   shape, and just at the point of the 'V' carve out a small indent
   into the wood.
3. The 30cm-long pole should be thinner than the bow, and it
   should be dry and of harder wood than the flat piece, as it will be
   used to create the friction and generate the heat.
4. Round off the end of this 30cm-long pole so that it fits snugly
   into the indent you cut previously.
5. Use the palm-sized piece to hold the 30cm-long pole
   in place.
6. Wrap the 30cm-long pole in the cord of the bow so that it's
   tightly held in the position you would fire an arrow from a bow.
   This is tricky and will require the help of a young apprentice.
7. Place the rounded end into the indent at the 'V' and gently hold it
   in place with the small piece of extra wood. Now apply pressure
   to the pole so it remains steady in place.
8. Start to move the bow back and forwards in a sawing motion.
   The tight cord should cause the pole to spin in place, moving it
   against the softer piece of wood on the bottom. With your own
   or your child's foot, hold that wood securely in place, and gently
   and consistently saw back and forth with the bow.

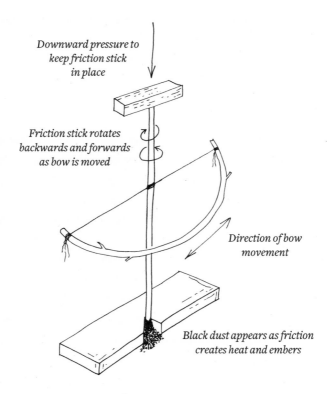

Downward pressure to
keep friction stick
in place

Friction stick rotates
backwards and forwards
as bow is moved

Direction of bow
movement

Black dust appears as friction
creates heat and embers

9. Nothing happens immediately, but gradually you'll start to see the wood blacken and eventually darkened sawdust will start to build up within the cut-out 'V'.

10. As you continue – and start sweating – hopefully, you'll begin to see smoke rising up right there in front of you. This is a great feeling and the perfect sign, as it shows that enough friction and heat are being produced.

11. Eventually, as the quantity of smoke builds, you'll begin to see tiny glowing embers in the black sawdust within the 'V'. This is the time to very gently add a tiny amount of tinder you've prepared by your side. Time is of the essence here, and if it

doesn't work first time – which it probably won't – try again, and again, and again ....

12. Eventually your tinder will catch alight with a very gentle bit of blowing. You'll see your first flame, you'll cheer with joy and very gently start adding the dry material you've collected. This is the start of your fire, the rewards of your patience and effort, and the start of your journey to becoming a fire-lighting expert. As you build the fire, feed it with more oxygen by blowing gently at the base. Fire always needs oxygen to burn, so don't be tempted to smother it with material – access to air is essential.

13. If something isn't working properly, try changing the type of wood you're using or alter the tension on the bow. If the drill feels as though there's no friction on the bottom plate of wood, try adding a few tiny grains of sand to the indent. This will instantly create friction and could make just the difference you need.

Lighting a fire this way is a very difficult process with a whole load of variables and moving parts that all have to be in sync for it to work. Ideally, all the wood should be dry, the right size and hardness, and the cord needs to be strong enough and under the correct tension. If you do manage to get an ember, then it's still really tricky to turn that into a flame from which a successful fire can grow. But when you do manage this, it's so rewarding for you together as a team and you'll have all connected back to your ancestral roots for a few minutes.

Fires do take time to build, they need nurturing, so if you add the fuel too soon you can smother a fire and put it out. Don't add the larger pieces of wood until you have a well-established heart of heat. It's so easy to see loads of big flames, believe that the fire is lit and then add large logs, only to discover you've killed it off. Heat is the key – develop the heat in the heart of the fire and the fuel can then be added at will.

There's a whole host of different methods you can use to try lighting your own fire. There are other friction methods using wood, sparks from flint and steel, and even chemical reactions using potassium permanganate crystals and glycerine. All of these can work, and some are much more challenging and time consuming than others. I'd suggest always carrying that box of matches to avoid disappointment, until your fire-lighting skills are those of an expert.

Challenge

Set challenges to see who can start a fire without artificial means. It's tough, takes time and hard work, but it's great fun and a fantastic experience for kids. These lessons that return us to our roots are really important and a source of pride to a young person when they know they have skills like this. Being able to light a fire by any means in any weather is a real talent and will always give you confidence when you're outdoors.

One of my very best and most vivid memories of camping at my grandparents' farm was being the first to wake up in the morning. Stiff, tired and most probably damp, I'd crawl out of my sleeping bag and head over to the campfire. There on the ground would be a pile of grey ash, and disappointment would flood over me as I realised we'd failed in our challenge of keeping the fire going for the whole of our stay. With a stick I'd flick back the ash just to check, and I'd see a couple of glowing embers embedded deep within. My spirits would instantly be lifted, and I'd grab some leaves that had curled up dry next to the burning flames the previous night. These crusty, dry pieces of tinder would be perfect to relight the fire, so I'd push them gently on to the embers.

Gradually, with a few breaths through my pursed lips directed towards the heat, the leaves would take and smoke would start to curl up before me. One more gentle blow would initiate the flames as the leaves burnt, and that was it – the life of the fire was now in my hands. Quickly I'd add some dry grass and as the flames grew I'd add some small thin twigs. The fire would come back to life, my cold fingers would start to feel warm again and move more freely, and the excitement would continue to rise within me. I'd add larger pieces of wood as the heat developed, and soon there was no doubt – I'd saved our fire for another day and the challenge was still on.

As I added wood, the crackling of the new fire became the camp's alarm clock and indicated breakfast time. My grandfather would roll awkwardly in his hammock swinging between two trees, then he'd sit back, rocking gently, and admire the fresh, cool morning mist over the lake in front of us. I like to believe those were his favourite moments in life. My dad would raise his head off the same old torn, dusty camp bed he'd been sleeping on right from childhood, and my brother Ali would appear from our tent or the rubber dinghy that he decided he wanted to sleep in that night. The cheery voice of my cousin Francis would ring out as the first voice of the day, congratulating me for bringing the fire back to life. He was always kind, he was a natural at this stuff and I admired him greatly for that. Over the course of two weeks each of us would take turns at bringing the fire back to life, each taking pride in the job, nurturing it after the cold night. It was always the best start to the day.

THE DAKOTA FIRE HOLE

This is an unusual but really fun way to build a fire. There are loads of elements here to engage the kids and turn having a fire into even more of an adventure than usual. The Dakota fire hole is great for a fairly discreet fire in a small space, leaving absolutely no trace behind you afterwards. The method does involve some 'construction' and takes a little time to prepare, but it's totally worth it when you get it going. It's also a really good way to cook food or boil water because of how it's set up.

What you need

+ A spade
+ Fire-lighting equipment – spark, tinder, kindling, fuel supply (you choose which method you use to create the spark, but for the purposes of this description I'll use matches)

What to do

1. Dig a hole in a suitable location to have your fire. This can even be done on the lawn in your garden because after the activity has finished the ground will look undisturbed.
2. The hole does not need to be big. The smaller it is, the less fuel you'll need to collect to burn – even the width of a standard garden spade will suffice.
3. Dig down to the depth of around 30cm.
4. Now dig another hole exactly the same depth and dimensions around 15 to 20cm away from your first hole.
5. Once you have two holes side by side, dig through to join the two holes, creating a tunnel under ground level. It's vital that you do not collapse the tunnel roof, so dig with care, as there needs to be two holes with an underground join.
6. Clear out any loose material.
7. Prepare the fire in one of the holes, laying out the tinder, kindling and fuel as you would for any fire.
8. Light the tinder and away you go!
9. Depending on several factors, you may need to increase the air flow into the fire initially by blowing gently down the empty hole

but once the heat builds and the fuel is burning you'll have a roaring fire.

10. The beauty of this is that the heat is contained within the four walls of the fire. This creates a beautifully hot fire that soon begins to feed itself with oxygen. As the fire burns, the hot air rises, sucking fresh air in via the empty hole through the joined tunnel and into the base of the fire. This of course stimulates the fire even more, creating a really robust, hot blaze. A hotter fire is more efficient, generating more heat and less smoke. I love this method too, because it's so discreet – you can't really see anything from a distance. All the flames are underground, so unless you're walking right past or spot a little bit of smoke you won't really know there's a fire burning there at all. At night, if you don't want to be seen while wild camping or need to evade the enemy, but you've still got to cook or have a fire to keep warm, then this is absolutely the fire for you.

11. Because the fire is underground, it makes it really easy to lay something over the top to cook on. A frying pan, for example, could be put right on the corners of the hole with the heat coming up from below, or it would be simple to spread a metal grate over the top and use that to cook on to your heart's content.

12. If we're using this fire hole in our garden I'll simply use a BBQ grate to cook on and rest a metal pan on the top to boil water for a cup of nettle tea (see page 108).

13. Out and about on a walk I'll often take a small square brass grill that I once cut from an old fire guard. It's great for creating a flat area to cook on or rest something on to boil water in.

14. Sticks can be pushed into the ground at angles over the heat, which rises straight up out of the hole, and kebabs or sausages can be cooked on them. If we head out to the countryside and decide to make a Dakota fire hole in the woods, I'll find two or

three really fresh, thick green branches and lay them over the top and rest my metal equipment for boiling water or cooking on top of them. Because they're thick and fresh, they won't burn well at all, and they'll still be strong and supporting for long after the cooking process has finished. There are literally so many options here to test out and try – the world is your oyster.

15. Once time is up, you've finished your cup of tea, cooked your dinner, had your fun with the fire hole and it's time to go home, then simply backfill the holes with the loose soil you previously dug out, even if the fire is still burning. This not only puts out the fire but also returns the ground to its previous state, leaving no trace other than perhaps a little loose soil. If you've done this on your lawn or in an area of grass, it's easy to remove a top layer of turf right at the start of the digging process. If you're careful and put it aside, you can then replace the turf afterwards and the grass will continue to grow as if nothing has happened. Actually, you know, it might even grow better than before with the ash you've buried containing phosphorus, potassium, calcium and other useful plant-growing elements.

What are the downsides to this fire? Well, to be honest, there can be a couple, depending on your circumstances. Sometimes the ground might be too hard, if it's frozen, or full of rocks or roots; it might even be too wet to dig down into to create a hole. You might also not have a spade to hand, which will make digging a fire hole pretty tricky. Holes can be dug using a stick or rocks, but this is hard work and very time consuming. As a challenge for kids, though, and if time is not an issue, it could be an even greater adventure, so give it a go.

If you need a fire to really warm yourselves on a cold day then this method probably isn't for you. It's absolutely brilliant for cooking on, but for heating people up, it's not great. You need to be very close to it

– or even right on top of it – to really get much warmth, as most of the heat is contained underground and shoots directly upwards.

Although it's a little more hard work than a normal fire, it's more efficient, so will require less fuel. This means fewer foraging trips for firewood, so the initial outlay of effort with the digging is offset later. Everyone should try making one – digging together, cooking together, having fun together over the awesome Dakota fire hole!

With a couple of hours to spare one Saturday afternoon I managed to haul the whole family out of the house. I'd been intending to make a Dakota fire hole for a number of weeks, as I hadn't built one for quite a while. We all traipsed out of the house bundled up in cold-weather gear and set off for the woods along a nearby footpath. By the time we made it to the location I'd been thinking of, two of the children were crying about having tired legs, all three were hungry, and I was getting agitated and just a little grumpy because time was ticking on. Hoping to snap them out of their moaning moods, I gave everyone a task to complete while I got to work digging the necessary holes.

It was a cold day, and the ground was icy and riddled with roots and flint. It took me much longer to dig than I'd expected, causing sweat to form on my brow and under my clothes. As I began to get asked how much longer I'd be, I could feel my mood changing to frustration, annoyance and anger. No one was collecting the wood I'd asked them to, the kids were messing around (having fun) and the hole still wasn't deep enough. So eventually I snapped.

The children's reaction was, of course, just to play up even more, and as I asked for assistance with rising anger, they helped less and less. My frustration grew until eventually I stood up, shouted, 'Right', and proceeded to fill in the hole I'd just spent nearly half an hour digging. Stamping down the loose rocks and earth, I kicked leaves over the disturbed ground, thrust the spade on to my shoulder and started to march off down the hill back home, announcing I'd see them all back there later. In the background, among the giggles, I could hear a little child's voice saying, 'Good'.

Things don't always go to plan. This time I let my frustration ruin the afternoon outside for everyone. I'd been put under pressure because my plan was too ambitious for the time frame we were working within. When you have kids things are liable to change – indeed circumstances can alter in an instant – so you have to be adaptable and willing to mould your day around them. It wasn't wrong that we attempted that project on that day, but I should have realised earlier that it wasn't realistic and chosen to do something different instead of getting cross. Climbing a beanstalk, making a walking stick or a spot of wildlife tracking would have been perfect.

COOK OVER A FIRE

Cooking over a fire is the best. The smoky flavour that wood smoke brings is, as we all know, something much sought after, even in Michelin-starred restaurants. So why not create your own restaurant outside on one of your adventures. I remember heading back to school as a youngster and telling my friends that we'd had our dinner cooked on a fire in the woods. No one believed me, but I was so excited and proud that we'd done something so unusual. It's the perfect thing to do on a summer's evening after school or on a warm weekend. It doesn't have to take long, but the thrill of heading out with a parent into the garden, woods or a suitable piece of land and starting a fire on which to cook dinner is something that will never be forgotten.

Jasper's campfire, by Jasper. We ate copious burnt
marshmallows, cooked over the flames from a packet as
big as him!

What you need

+ Fire-lighting equipment
+ A frying pan/metal container/grill
+ Food to be cooked
+ A knife
+ An oven glove/damp cloth, to protect hands

What to do

1. Light a fire in a suitable location.
2. Once the fire has been built and a good supply of glowing
   embers has formed, cooking can begin.

3. Flatten out the embers and lay the frying pan or other metal cooking utensil on top.

4. Keep a close watch throughout the cooking process – resting objects on fires can be dangerous. As the wood burns it will move, potentially causing accidents.

5. There are endless complicated set-ups you can invent using sticks, rocks, wire – anything non-flammable you can find – but a couple of green logs placed on either side of the embers is pretty good for resting a frying pan or a metal pot on.

6. When moving cooking utensils, consider how you're going to hold the cooking pot and its metal handle once they're hot. An oven glove or damp cloth will be needed – there's nothing worse than painfully burnt hands when trying to have a good time!

It wasn't so long ago that I was lucky enough to be invited on an adventure holiday to Croatia. We were to be based on a sailing boat and would explore the Dalmatian coast while sea kayaking, sailing and mountain biking on and around some of the most beautiful islands you can imagine. It was out of the normal tourist season, so the whole place was deserted, and there were hundreds of miles of coastline to explore.

A couple of days into the trip we were met by a young local man who came swimming out to us and clambered aboard our boat. He worked on the mainland at the local university in the sports department but was also well known as a very good chef with a family background in traditional Croatian cooking. Tonight we'd be feasting from his hand. I'd heard great things and was hugely looking forward to the forthcoming meal.

We moored up on the island of Hvar, loaded our gear on to bikes and set off up the winding mountain roads. The island has a long history of human habitation and as we cycled, marvelling at the views under bright blue skies, our tour guide told us about the island's rich past.

Finally, as the sun started to set in the western sky and the temperature dropped, we arrived at the idyllic rustic farmhouse in which we'd be spending the night. Perched high on a hillside, this recently renovated farmhouse looked on to the mainland in the distance. Over the stone-walled fields and olive groves, and out across the calm sea, we could see every detail before us. We were transported back to a time when farmers lived a subsistence lifestyle up there, growing all their own vegetables, raising their animals for meat and selling the small amount of olive oil they pressed by their own hand. It truly was a fascinating place.

The chef, however, wasted no time looking at the view. He immediately got to work lighting the fire in the ancient hearth, and within minutes there was a roaring blaze and the heat began to penetrate the room. He wasn't messing around – his intention was to get the fire hot enough and in the right state for cooking as quickly as possible, and he fed armful after armful of wood into the blazing inferno.

While the fire was burning down to the right state for cooking, the young chef prepared a huge leg of lamb, expertly removing the meat from the bone, then he diced and seasoned the vegetables, all of which he put into an enormous metal cooking pan along with a handful of rosemary picked from the walled garden right in front of the house. With all the ingredients packed into the pot, the lid was placed on top and pushed right into the middle of the embers, with only the very top of the lid visible. I was intrigued, as the speed of the whole process so far had been astounding. But now was the time to sit back and relax, have a drink, talk and wait for the meal to be ready.

It took a couple of hours. Every now and then the dying embers would be thrown back over the pot to maintain the heat, and about two hours after he'd started the chef jumped up and confidently pulled the pot from the fire. I couldn't understand how he knew whether it would be ready or not, but his actions were so definite and confident that I was sure it was all going to be wonderful. Blowing the ash carefully off the lid, he heaved the whole thing on to a piece of wood in the centre of the table and began to serve out the steaming feast. The aroma spread through the room and everyone without fail started salivating. The wait was over and the food absolutely didn't disappoint. The lamb fell apart on our plates, tender, moist and delicious, and the vegetables were all faultlessly cooked, soft and sweet, with a hint of rosemary. I'd never seen anything like it before – the simplest of cooking methods, with food cooked to utter perfection.

Tucking into something you've cooked yourself over a fire is incredibly rewarding. I'll always remember the fried breakfasts my grandfather cooked over the fire in that battered old black frying pan that had only ever been washed in a stream. I don't suppose they were particularly healthy, but my goodness they were delicious. The centre of our camp was always around the fire, and we'd all finish our days by clambering into our sleeping bags stinking of wood smoke. I recall that for some reason my grandfather named the camp 'Smokey Joe's'. The 'smokey' part was obvious, but we didn't know anyone called Joe ...

CAMPFIRE RECIPES

SMOKEY JOE'S FRY-UP

Serves 2–3

What you need

+ A little vegetable oil
+ 4 sausages
+ 4 rashers of bacon

+ 4 eggs
+ 10 small mushrooms
+ 4 tomatoes
+ 4 slices of bread

What to do

1. As rustic as it comes, start by frying the sausages in a few drops of vegetable oil in the frying pan nestled into the fire's embers.
2. Once the sausages are golden, add the bacon until cooked on one side. Flip them over, then crack the eggs into the pan in the gaps between the sausages and bacon.
3. In any other available gaps add the mushrooms and tomatoes, which should all get drawn in and connected by the egg white.
4. Continue to fry until everything is cooked to taste.
5. Cut up the food into portions in the frying pan and slide each portion out on to a plate. Quickly add the bread to the pan with a little more vegetable oil. Fry both sides and add to the plate when golden brown and crisp. The most delicious, crusty, smoky breakfast right there in the fresh air – what a fantastic way to start the day!

Of course, this is just one simple recipe – but it's a great start. A full stomach in preparation for a night under the stars or a day of adventure is just what we all need. Tweak this recipe to suit your needs and become familiar with cooking over a fire – it does take a bit of getting used to, but the results will improve with practice. We won't all be as good as my friend the Croatian chef, who was indeed a natural and who instinctively knew, after years of practice and experience, what would be happening to his food and when.

FIRESIDE BANANA PANCAKES

Serves 2

I love them, my kids love them, everyone loves them! We make these pancakes indoors, outdoors and everywhere we go. This is the easiest way to make a pancake – it's almost unbelievably simple.

What you need

+ Fire/stove
+ A bowl or bag to mix the ingredients
+ A fork to mash the banana
+ 2 medium-sized bananas
+ 2 eggs
+ A frying pan/baking tray

What to do

1. Mash and mix two medium-sized bananas with two eggs. This can be done in a bowl or even in a plastic sandwich bag while outdoors. Be careful not to pierce the bag if that's the way you choose to do it.
2. Pour the ingredients into the pre-heated frying pan or baking tray, aiming to make small pancakes 5cm in diameter.
3. Heat the mixture for a minute on one side until it becomes golden brown and crispy, then flip it over. This can be tricky, and these pancakes sometimes don't hold together as well as pancakes made from flour. Don't worry. If the mixture breaks and crumbles, it's easy to re-form the pancake into the right shape when all the ingredients are cooked.

4. The pancakes are ready to eat once golden brown on both sides. The beauty of these pancakes, apart from their simplicity and the few ingredients required, is that they are naturally sweet. So although it's nice to add syrup or honey, it's really quite unnecessary. This truly is a healthy super-quick, easy fun snack to have outdoors. Time to tuck in and enjoy!

CAMPFIRE POPCORN

Serves 2

There's so much going on for the senses with this simple recipe that I really think it's a must to try with the kids. Not only do you get the benefit of a healthy, delicious popcorn snack that everyone loves, but there's also the excitement and expectation of something moving and popping right in front of your eyes. It's very uncomplicated, requiring just a few basic ingredients and a fire – and away you go!

What you need

+ 4 tbsp popcorn kernels
+ 2 tbsp vegetable oil
+ A small plastic ziplock sandwich bag
+ Tin foil

What to do

1. Before heading outside, put the popcorn kernels and the oil into a small plastic ziplock sandwich bag or something similar so that the oil and kernels mix up perfectly on your walk. Make sure

the bag is done up properly, as the last thing you need is an oil leak in your pocket.

2. Once the campfire is lit, tip out the oiled kernels in to the middle of a sheet of tin foil, leaving plenty of space around the edge. Lay another piece of foil over the top and fold up all the edges, creating a sealed package with plenty of space in the middle for the popcorn to expand.

3. Carefully place the package at the edge of the fire, just brushing the heat. Listen and watch – as the package gets hot, the first kernels will begin to pop and you may even see the foil package move. Once the popping becomes regular, twist the package over with a stick so a different side is exposed to the heat. Gradually and carefully expose each edge to the heat. Soon all the kernels will have popped and turned into your delicious popcorn.

4. It takes a little experimentation and judgement to get this absolutely right, as the time it takes for the popcorn to be ready will depend on the size and heat of your fire. Do be extremely careful when opening the foil package – the contents will be hot. Now sit round with the open foil bag in front of you all and share this delicious outdoor snack!

BREAD ON A STICK

Serves 2

Damper bread is a very simple traditional Australian bread made historically by those travelling or working in the outback. The bread was originally developed by stockmen, who would travel for long periods of time with very basic rations. Flour, water and sometimes milk were used, and the dough was cooked in the ashes of the fire. My suggestion would be to cook the bread on sticks over a fire, each

Jasper, Daisy and Jesse cooking dinner over a fire, by Daisy.

person cooking their own little stick of damper bread. It's such a
fun thing to do, and although it's very simple it will probably take a
couple of attempts to get it just right. This is a great outdoor-cooking
activity, with a number of skills being put to the test.

What you need

+ 1 large mixing bowl
+ 1 cup of self-raising flour
+ 1 tbsp butter
+ A pinch of salt
+ 1 tsp sugar
+ ½ cup of milk
+ 2 long, fresh green sticks

What to do

1. It's best to make the dough before heading outdoors. It can
   easily be transported in sandwich bags, ready to get out at
   the fireside.

2. Mix the flour and the butter thoroughly until the mixture becomes crumbly.

3. Add the salt and sugar, then gradually add a little milk until it forms a good dough. If the mixture becomes too sticky, add a little more flour. Eventually you should be able to form a clean ball of dough in your hand.

4. Divide the dough into two equal-sized balls and roll out into snake shapes.

5. Twist the dough around the sticks and place above the hot embers. Try not to put the bread into the flames, as the bread will blacken and burn, and won't cook inside. Instead, as you would with a BBQ, wait for the fire to die down until only the embers remain.

6. The cooking process may take 20 to 30 minutes, the slower the better. Make sure you regularly twist the stick over the heat, so all sides of the dough come into contact with the heat and the bread is cooked evenly. The dough will gradually turn into golden and delicious bread twists, something your child will be very proud of and excited to eat.

This is a brilliantly simple recipe for making a tasty and filling outdoor fireside snack. Adding raisins to the dough will give the damper bread a sweetness, and you can place them in the twists to look like caterpillar's eyes! Once children start to learn how simple bread-making can be, they'll gain a great deal of confidence to try other methods and experiment both outdoors and at home in the kitchen. I certainly grew up thinking bread was a really complex process. No doubt it can be, but it can also be exceedingly simple and enjoyable.

Challenge

Depending on the time of year, different foraged foods can be added to the food you cook on a fire. Autumn is a fantastic season because you can add blackberries gathered from the hedgerows, as well as crushed-up hazelnuts, if you manage to collect them before the squirrels get to them. These simple recipes really do make getting outdoors for a couple of hours and cooking over a fire easy and fun!

CREATE A FOOTPRINT TRAP

It fascinates me to think about what goes on right under our noses at night. Most of us have no idea what is out there in our gardens or in our parks, scurrying about, sniffing around in the quiet hours of darkness. Maybe you don't want to know, but I can assure you that your kids do ...

Here's a great activity to make something so that you can discover what's out there. It's fun, exciting and really interesting when you find a spot that does indeed have after-dark wild-animal traffic. An important thing to learn here is the virtue of patience, as you'll have to wait until the next day or even longer to see the results. It's always a risk that the kids will lose interest if they don't see instant results – and sometimes that does happen – but it will be down to you to build up their interest and wonder while the construction process is under way. Sometimes it's good to do things that force us to wait, things that will give us satisfaction but not immediately, as so many of us are becoming expectant and reliant on instant results and gratification. This activity is perfect in that regard.

What you need

+ 1 large piece of COREX/foldable rigid plastic, 60 ×100cm
+ Duct tape
+ 2 pieces of white A4 paper
+ Masking tape
+ A small flat dish, 5cm in diameter (such as a plant-pot saucer/ jam-jar lid)
+ Powdered poster paint (preferably black)
+ 1 tbsp vegetable oil
+ Dry cat food/dog food/something without salt or sugar, to entice animals

What to do

1. Fold the COREX board into a triangle so that it forms a tunnel. Try to make sure that each side of the tunnel wall is the same size, so that it forms an even triangular tunnel. The tubular make-up of COREX helps with this and makes an even fold easy.
2. Tape the join of the COREX securely with duct tape to maintain the tunnel shape.
3. Line the floor of tunnel with the A4 paper and secure it with masking tape.
4. Fill the dish in the centre of the tunnel with cat food or your chosen bait.
5. At either end of the tunnel place two strips of masking tape, side by side on the paper. Stick them down.
6. Mix up the poster-paint powder with the vegetable oil until it creates a thick paint and spread it thickly on to the strips of masking tape. This is where the animal should pick up paint on its feet as it walks towards the food, leaving footprints on the

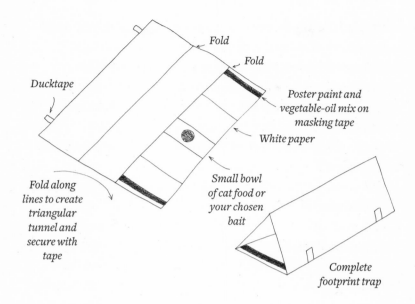

Fold

Fold

Ducktape

Poster paint and
vegetable-oil mix on
masking tape

White paper

Fold along
lines to create
triangular
tunnel and
secure with
tape

Small bowl
of cat food or
your chosen
bait

Complete
footprint trap

paper. The reason vegetable oil is used is not only because it's non-toxic to animals if they try to lick it off their feet – it also stays wet for a number of days. This will enable you to leave the trap out and give maximum time for success.

7. The footprint trap is now set. Carefully place it in a hidden part of the garden – in a flowerbed, under a tree, next to a fence or along a track that you already know animals frequent – and wait overnight.

8. Hopefully, the next morning, you and your child can head out to see what has been in the trap. It will be obvious if something has been inside, as there will be footprints on the white paper.

It's amazing what you can discover, and it really will give you an insight into the sorts of creatures that are out and about in your vicinity during the night. If you do this regularly, you can start to build up a picture of what is living in close proximity to you.

When children see this their imaginations are sparked. Small mammal footprints are incredibly interesting – each one has slightly different foot shapes and prints, and some are just incredibly sweet! (See pages 88–9.) Knowing these vulnerable creatures with their little footprints are there near you is something to embrace. If you're lucky, you may get some really clean and clear prints, so why not turn them into a framed picture on your child's bedroom wall.

Challenge

There's a huge amount of useful technology out there that makes spotting daytime or nocturnal wildlife much easier. If you have the budget, take a look at night-vision cameras or wildlife-specific camera traps. These are readily available online and both can give incredible footage of wildlife.

Camera traps are weather-proof cameras housed within a rugged box that can be secured to a tree or fence post. When an animal – or human – walks in front of the trap, the camera is automatically set off and starts recording. Nowadays, these cameras can operate during both night and day. They produce amazing results, and, most importantly, do not disturb the wildlife.

This activity takes time and patience, but it's unbelievably rewarding when it works and animals are seen to have been in the trap. It helps give children a greater awareness of the creatures that live alongside them, ones that they've probably never seen before. If they're aware that these animals are there, they're more likely to be interested in them, and therefore more likely to care about and gain an understanding of them.

I've noticed with my youngest boy, Jesse, that he wants feedback instantly. If he's watching a programme on TV and it finishes, he wants something on again instantly. If there's a programme loading up on YouTube that he wants to watch (yes, he does watch YouTube!) and it doesn't start playing immediately, he'll move straight on to the next programme. His attention span is short and his patience is low. It seems to be increasingly common with the instant gratification we're now used to getting in our online lives. It's social change at an extremely fast pace, and leads to frustration if the things we come to expect don't materialise.

MAKE A WOODEN WHISTLE

Sometimes you need a relaxed day getting lost in an activity while outside in the fresh air. If I was ever tired from training, which was all the time, and if my legs were aching and deeply fatigued and I didn't have the energy to walk for miles or go for a bike ride, I'd try to find a weekend-afternoon activity that I could do with the kids that took us outside, gave the kids the fresh air they needed but also allowed me a little rest. This activity is perfect in all these respects. It needs very little preparation and equipment, you don't have to travel, and you can do it sitting down in the grass, on a riverbank, on a tree stump in the woods or outside the back door of your house. It's a sedate activity that requires care and skill, but it's rewarding and satisfying on completion.

What you need

+   A straight stick of sycamore, 12cm long and 1.5cm in diameter. (The sycamore tree can be identified by its five-pointed leaf, and later in the year by the 'helicopter' seeds it produces.)
+   A small, sharp penknife

What to do

1. Cut your stick of sycamore from a tree. It must be fresh, green wood.
2. Make sure that the cut ends are free from splits and splinters, and that the stick is as straight as possible.
3. Lie the stick on a flat, solid surface and about 3cm from one end cut directly down into the stick about halfway through, to make a straight-line cut into the wood.
4. Cut an angle in the wood towards that vertical cut from 0.5cm away. This should create a chip in the stick, which starts to form your whistle opening.
5. These cuts in the wood should be done extremely carefully. Try to make the edges as clean and precise as you can. Children will need help with this, which makes it the perfect activity to really bond over.
6. Now carefully cut a mouthpiece in the end of the stick that is closest to the cut you've just made. It's simply scraping away the wood on the underside of the whistle to create a recorder-like mouthpiece.
7. Measure around 5cm down from the angle cut you just made in the top of the whistle and score a mark right around the circumference of the stick. This cut should go through the bark

layer but not cut right through the stick. It should be done very
carefully right around the stick.

8. Now with the handle of the knife or a larger piece of wood,
   very carefully beat the stick, tapping it all around. It's really
   important to take this stage slowly and not bang the wood with
   too much pressure. You're just trying to bruise the bark of the
   stick, which will release the sap inside. This will in turn enable
   the layer of bark to slide off your whistle, revealing the wood
   inside. It's important not to damage the bark, however, so do
   gauge the right amount of pressure. I'd say it should be the
   same pressure you would use to tap a nail into a soft piece of
   plasterboard on a wall.

9. When you notice the bark looking wet, which is the sap escaping,
   it's time to grasp the bark and with gentle pressure twist and
   pull. The bark should then simply slide off the stick, revealing
   the clean white wood underneath. This may take a bit of

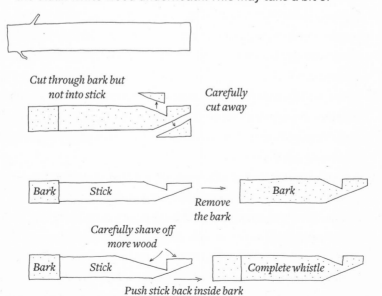

Cut through bark but not into stick

Carefully cut away

Bark | *Stick*

Remove the bark

Bark

Carefully shave off more wood

Bark | *Stick*

Complete whistle

Push stick back inside bark

pressure and a bit more of the beating. Take your time with this
and don't force it with undue pressure. If you break the bark,
you'll have to start all over again.

10. Now carefully shave off a couple of millimetres of wood from
the mouthpiece to the top of the start of the vertical cut. You're
looking to create a flat top to the wood.

11. It's time now time to very, very carefully deepen the angled cut
you made previously. It's important to keep the edges really
clean and precise, so make small carvings, take your time, and
help any youngster when they are doing this. The idea is to
create a longer, less angled cut to the wood.

12. Keep the vertical cut in exactly the same place, while increasing
the depth of the angled cut. You're trying to achieve a large
cavity in this section of the inside of the whistle.

13. Push the knife carefully all the way to the vertical cut and keep
doing this until there is a couple of inches of angle.

14. Be very careful not to cut all the way through the stick. If that
happens, you'll have to start again from the beginning. There's
no repairing these mistakes, and the whole process requires
precision.

15. This section takes time. You're trying to create as much space
between the vertical cut and the start of the angled cut as you
can. This will form the chamber or cavity inside your whistle,
around which the air will flow.

16. Once you're happy that all the edges are cleanly cut and
precise, slide on the tube of bark that you previously slid
off. Be extremely careful with this delicate piece of the
whistle. Any breaks in the bark might cause the whistle not
to work.

17. Once the bark is back on, in place, and the cut sections are
lined up, give it a blow. Hopefully, if all the cuts have been done

carefully, cleanly and accurately, a loud whistle should
come out from the stick you're holding in your hand.
How exciting!

This activity is a brilliant one to do with children, as long as you
don't mind the sound of a whistle ringing through the house for ever
more! It's an activity that involves going out and finding the correct
materials, careful control with a knife, and working together, as you'll
have to help your child with the cutting. Care needs to be taken at
all stages, and the process involves thought, communication and
patience. The result is a fantastic fun tool that gives the satisfaction
of crafting something together.

Please be patient with this – it's worth pursuing and giving
it a few goes, as it rarely works first time. But once you know
the basic technique and where the cuts go, it doesn't take long.
You can also experiment with the size of the hollow chamber
inside the whistle, which will alter the pitch and sound of
your whistle.

BIRDWATCHING

If you were to make an appearance on *Mastermind*, what would you
choose as your specialist subject? I've thought about this often, but
I don't know many topics in depth, to be honest, which sometimes
worries me. If I were pushed to make a decision, I'd have to go with
British birds. I'm certainly not an expert, but I do know my robins
from my blackbirds, so I think I'd stand up OK on the subject, to start
with at least!

A robin with a tasty worm, by Jasper.

My bird knowledge has grown over the years, alongside my interest in wildlife. What birds really are was brought home to me as a 12 year old, when I gained my first accidental pet bird (see page 163). The love I acquired for her certainly made me much more aware of the habits and needs of birds, as well as the different bird species in this country.

Birds are easily affected by the actions of human beings. From the reduction of the areas available for their nesting sites to the disappearance of their food sources, they're creatures that we can harm without directly intending to, but they're also easy animals to help and encourage. A small amount of effort on our part can make a huge difference to them.

What you need

+   Bird food. There's a huge range of bird food available, catering
    for many different species of bird. A mixed seed selection with
    added mealworms is ideal and will feed the greatest range of
    garden birds.
+   A bird feeder (optional)

What to do

1. Head into your garden or, if you don't have one, into a park or
   outdoor space. Wherever you are outside in the world, you're
   more than likely to see a bird flying around.
2. Listen out for them and watch their movement.
3. Put bird food in your bird feeder, or if you're in a park or
   outdoor space, scatter a handful on the ground some distance
   from you.
4. Sit somewhere slightly hidden – on a bench, on a cushion on
   the ground, or in a tent. Wherever you are, ensure you have a
   good view of the place you've scattered the bird food, and watch
   which birds arrive, how they act and what they eat – even
   how they eat. From your little hidden sanctuary, you and your
   child can discuss what you notice, jot down some notes and
   identify the most common birds using a bird-identification book
   or app.
5. If you do have a bird feeder in your garden and keep it regularly
   topped up, you'll notice a constant population of birds accessing
   it and feeding from it. The moment you stop filling up the feeder
   or remove it completely, these birds will stop visiting and you'll
   immediately notice a difference. The problem is, once you start
   providing food the birds do start to become a little reliant on you,

and if there's excess quantity provided they might be reluctant to forage for themselves.

6. My take on it would be to provide a modest amount consistently. They'll visit you often but won't rely on you, and so they'll have to support themselves too, and if you can't supply any food for a while it won't hit them so hard. The beauty of providing food for your local population of birds is that you'll definitely be helping them.

7. Once you start feeding the birds, more will come, as birds learn very quickly where they can access sources of food.

8. Winter is a vital time in which to feed birds, as their natural food sources become increasingly scarce.

This activity is so simple and can take as much or as little effort as you'd like it to. If you have the time, space and the opportunity, you can certainly combine a number of activities in this book with this one. For example, build your own den (see page 218) and then head

Jasper and Daddy birdwatching, by Jasper. An airborne battle between two red kites, fighting ferociously over a dead rabbit.

into it after school with a hot drink and share some restful, quiet time together outdoors. If your den is built in an easily accessible place, then keep a supply of bird food in a bird feeder near by. Then when you decide to visit, there will already be birds around. Birds often don't react to voices if they see no movement, so you can happily chat in a self-made shelter while observing your new-found garden friends.

Challenge

It's easy to buy ready-made bird boxes with video cameras housed inside. This technology is incredible, is readily available online and enables you to watch wild birds up close. I highly recommend putting up one of these bird boxes in your garden – or against the wall of a building close to you – and connecting it to your TV so that you can follow the lives of your local birds. If you get the timing right, and put the bird box in place early enough in the season, and you're lucky, the birds will choose your box to nest in.

It's difficult to describe how interesting it is watching a pair of tiny blue tits or similar going through the nesting phases, from building the nest, laying a clutch of eggs, incubating them and, finally, the most exciting bit, feeding the young. Without disturbing the birds, you have direct and constant access to their lives – look out of the window and you can see them flying to your feeder, look back to your screen and you can see them in the nest! It's well worth the cost.

It all began outside the back door of our family cottage in a small village in Worcestershire. As I stepped outside I heard a tiny chirping sound from low down on the ground. My interest immediately piqued, I took to my hands and knees, only to discover the tiniest little

hatchling bird I'd ever seen. It can't have been any more than a few
days old, pink and featherless, and it was completely helpless down
there on the paving slabs. I was overcome with the need to rescue this
little life.

My mum and I tried to find out where it had come from, intending
to put it back in its nest. We found it after a bit of searching around,
but it was tucked deep under the roof tiles in a tiny crack. There was no
way we were going to be able to get this little thing back in there, so we
made the decision to keep it and try to raise it ourselves. Even then, at
the age of 12, I knew it wasn't the best option, and that this chick
would be far better off with its own parents providing for it and
raising it. It was too young and delicate, and we'd never done this
before, so its chances of survival were extremely slim. But at that point
we couldn't see another way – if we left it where it was it was sure to die
very quickly.

Some might say that that's nature's way and it's the way it should
be, but I have difficulty with this notion. If you've exhausted all options
of getting it back to its nest and its mother, and the only alternative is to
leave it where it is, then I don't believe that's the best course of action.
Our impact on the natural environment is everywhere and I believe we
affect nearly everything in it, so when the question of rescuing a bird in
danger arises I'm all for it.

Mum and I set about trying to feed this little thing. Worms were
obviously the first point of call – all birds eat worms, right? Well,
apparently this one didn't. Not even dangling a juicy wriggling worm
freshly plucked from the soil would tempt this little chap to open its
beak. So perhaps it preferred them mashed? This is something I'm
not proud of – and I remember finding it hard to do – but I mashed
up a worm in a bowl with a spoon and tried to feed this tiny chick.
Disgusting! We either had the fussiest baby bird on the planet or, as we
soon found out, sparrows prefer a diet of grains and seeds.

Without an immediate supply of seeds, we somehow stumbled on the idea of scrambled egg. Whether or not it was my breakfast that morning, we can't now remember, but as we offered the chick a spoonful of warm scrambled egg it instantly devoured it. We'd found the answer – by some strange irony these birds have a penchant for scrambled egg and, in this case, absolutely nothing else.

I assumed responsibility for the care of this little bird and I took my role very seriously indeed. It was my goal to keep it alive, so I was happy to use whatever means necessary. I started to learn that when it refused to eat, a good trick was to hold some scrambled egg between my thumb and forefinger, and use my hand to act like a bird flying into the nest with my fingers flapping on one side like wings. It would then be more likely to sit back and open its beak, enabling me to drop a good portion of egg down its throat. Early on we made the mistake of providing warm scrambled egg, so it wasn't long before it started to insist that its egg was always warm – not so useful when you're in a rush or only have leftovers. But we got by.

Over the course of a few weeks the bird grew considerably and became much more accustomed to my clumsy feeding methods. As its feathers started to grow we discovered she was a female house sparrow. We called her Sparky. I'd leave her during the day while at school, then return to find her in her 'nest' – a small picnic basket – starving and desperate for company. Out she'd come and make her way on to my shoulder, where she'd sit happily, tucked into my neck for warmth. As she grew she began to learn to fly. More and more I'd notice she was spreading her wings, using them to balance as I walked around with her on my shoulder or in my hand. Any sudden movements would cause her to flap and regain her balance. I quickly realised this was her method of learning to fly, so I'd sit her on my finger and drop my hand down, slowly at first, then through the week speed up the drop. I'd change directions of my hand movements to give her variety and test her. Before long she was flying herself, landing roughly back in my hand. I'd often have to catch her in those early days, but she was starting to learn. It was amazing to see this process, although I didn't necessarily appreciate just how fascinating it was at that age.

Sparky quickly became my best mate. During the day she'd live in the garden, flying from tree to tree, the sound of her 'chirp' ringing out constantly as she called for me. When I stepped outside and called her name she'd fly down from a perch in the apple tree, swoop down to my shoulder and nestle into my neck. I'd pick her up and throw her back into the tree, walk away, call her name and she'd fly right back to me. It really was an amazing bond between us – perhaps it was more of a bond for me and simply a relationship of convenience for her. I was her provider of warmth and food, but I prefer to think she liked me. We continued to feed her scrambled eggs and for a good couple of years she lived happily in this way. Then one fateful day when I returned from school she was nowhere to be found. I called and called, sat outside and waited. It was so unlike her, but she never came. She didn't come for her warm scrambled egg that night, and she didn't come when the sun set below the horizon. Sparky was gone.

Unfortunately, perhaps the problem was caused by my hand rearing or 'imprinting' of a wild bird. Imprinting is where a human being or other animal acts as a wild animal's mother and they grow up to believe this to be the case. They learn everything from their mother, which in human–wild-animal relationships can cause serious problems. A wild mother would teach their young fear and wariness, and to fly off whenever a predator was near. I never taught her that. From me she knew to trust everything. She was completely fearless. We'll never know for sure but we think she was fearless towards the next-door neighbour's cat and sadly met her end on the other side of the hedge. It was a sad time for me – Sparky had been

my friend, I loved her! – but I'd learnt so much not only about house
sparrows but also about wild animals in general, how they interact
and how they learn.

Anyone who knows me well will have heard this story. I'd bore my
teammates to death on training camps with it and they'd all take the
mickey asking if any bird we saw was Sparky. I didn't mind – it was
funny and I think they all found it pretty amazing, really. From then
on, I had a far better understanding of birds, so I now do my very best
to teach and encourage my children to have an interest in them and
feed them. It's incredibly easy and costs virtually nothing. Birds are
beautiful little creatures that do us no harm in any way, and so in my
mind there's no reason not to support them.

MAKE AN EASY BIRD FEEDER

What you need

+ A penknife
+ An empty screwtop plastic bottle
+ A length of string
+ A plastic paint-pot lid, or similar
+ Some birdseed

What to do

1. Pierce two small holes in the base of the bottle and thread
   some string through. It's even better if this is string you've made
   yourself (see 'Make string', page 31).

2. Tie the ends of the string together to create a loop, on which you can eventually hang up the feeder.
3. Cut a hole in the base of the plastic lid exactly the same circumference as the opening of the bottle. As accurate a cut as possible is ideal, as there shouldn't be any gaps between the lid and the bottle.
4. Push the bottle opening through the hole and screw on the lid underneath, so the bottle is standing upside down and the lid is the correct way up.
5. The lid should now be secure and stable.
6. Now very carefully cut three small upside-down triangles in the plastic bottle close to the lid. These will be the holes the seed falls out of to land in the lid.
7. Unscrew the cap of the bottle that's under the plastic lid and fill the bottle with birdseed, then replace the cap. (See if you can do this without spilling any – I never can!)
8. Now hang the feeder from a tree branch, bird table or fence.
9. The seed will spill out of the cut holes in the bottle and fall into the small plastic lid, so that birds will be able to land on the lid edge and feed.
10. Try to place the feeder in a fairly open spot. Birds are shy creatures, with an innate sensitivity to the threat of predators. If the feeder is too close to undergrowth or a hedge, the birds will be less likely to use it.
11. Make sure the feeder is in clear view of your hiding place. There's nothing worse than forcing yourself into uncomfortable positions and straining to see something for a couple of hours.

Challenge

Take photos, draw pictures and write notes on the birds and wildlife you observe. If you can encourage your child to do some of these things at a young age – and to do so while spending time with you – it's precious time spent together that will inevitably be helpful to them in their growth and development. Observation, description, writing, research, knowledge, art, understanding and appreciation of the natural world are just some of the benefits of this activity. I'm not suggesting it's always going to be calm, relaxed and easy. Sometimes the mood you're both in will be right – at other times it won't be. That's fine and to be expected. But giving yourselves the opportunity is crucial.

BUILD A BAT BOX

Bats struggle with nesting sites. Nowadays we convert barns, seal up cracks and gaps in our houses, cut down dead trees, manicure our gardens and remove those beautifully rugged, rough old ponds that used to provide a food source for them. Bats need our help, and one way is to provide nesting sites for them to roost in and hibernate. Because they swoop and climb into their nesting sites, the make-up of the box needs to be specific – a standard bird box won't do at all!

What you need

+ A tape measure
+ A pencil

+ Untreated rough-sawn wood, roughly 15cm wide, 1.1 metre long, and 1.5cm thick
+ A saw
+ Screws or nails

What to do

1. Measure along the edge of the wood and draw lines across each mark. We are measuring the bat-box sides here, which will then be cut: *Backplate – 33cm, Front – 14cm, Base – 9cm, Lid – 20cm, Side 1 – 20cm along one edge, 14cm on the other, Side 2 – 14cm along one edge, 20cm along the other.*

2. Cut out all the edges to the lengths stated above. You and your child can share this – measuring, drawing the lines, cutting out and preparing the wood to be screwed together into a box shape.

3. Take the backplate and, using the saw, roughen up the wood so that the bats are able to climb up through a gap and grip on. A smooth-sanded piece of wood is useless for this.

4. You can cut horizontal grooves in the wood, if you prefer, making something of a ladder for the bats, starting right at the bottom of the backplate and leading right to the top. Alternatively, you could staple some hessian sack, thin cork board or even sandpaper on to the backplate.

5. It's really important to source some untreated wood, because bats are sensitive to chemicals and can die if exposed to treated wood. Bats also hate draughts, so the joins in this construction must be tight and secure. This requires a little accuracy, so guidance on the cutting and fitting will be important!

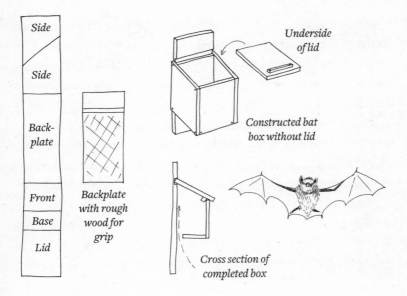

Underside of lid

Constructed bat box without lid

Side

Side

Back-plate

Front

Base

Lid

Backplate with rough wood for grip

Cross section of completed box

6. Once all the pieces are cut out, screw or nail them carefully together, ensuring all the joins are as tight as can be. Keeping water and draughts out is really important.

7. Decide on the location. This could be high up on a wall against the side of your house, under the roof eaves to make it even more weather-protected, or high up in a tree. If screwing into a wall, make sure the box is secure and safe by using wall plugs and deep screws. If your chosen site is up a tree, use adjustable ties or specialised timber-screw bolts to reduce damage to the tree itself.

8. Once the box is in position it's not legally allowed to be opened without a licence, as bats are protected mammals. This is one reason why bat boxes do not have lids that open.

It may take no time at all, or it might take years for bats to populate your new box. This activity is about creating a safe and secure environment that you and your kids care about. If bats do discover your box and the positioning is correct, it's likely they'll stay there for many years. If you're really lucky, they might even breed there. In conjunction with your bat detector (see page 68), much of the year you'll be enjoying these little creatures, understanding and appreciating them even more. Sitting outside on a summer's evening, or sleeping out in the back garden with your bat detector switched on, listening to them out hunting, is a special thing to do.

BUILD A HEDGEHOG HOUSE

There's so much that goes on under the cover of darkness that we know very little about. There's a whole other world outside when the sun goes down; as we're curled up warm in our beds, our gardens and surroundings come to life in a very different way from in the daytime. Most of the time we've no idea about the wild

A hedgehog, by Jasper. They have enormous noses in our garden.

creatures that surround us at night, going about their business, but sometimes we're lucky enough to come across our nocturnal neighbours.

Hedgehogs don't require much – a very simple shelter will give them just the helping hand they need. A rough area of garden with a big pile of twigs, cut branches and leaves is perfect, but an old upturned basket filled with leaves or straw could be ideal too. Something more robust like an upturned half barrel with an entrance cut out would make a safe and secure palace.

What you need

+ A saw
+ An old wooden box/crate
+ Some plastic sheeting, enough to cover the top of the box at the very least
+ Straw/hay/dry leaves

What to do

1. Carefully saw an arch shape into the rim of one edge of the wooden box.
2. Turn the box open-side down to check the opening is large enough for a hedgehog to crawl in – 15cm along the base and the same height should be perfect.
3. Place the box in the area of the garden or land that you want the hedgehog house to go. The less disturbed and the more hidden, the better.
4. Cover the top of the upturned box in plastic sheeting to waterproof it. There's no need to completely cover the sides.

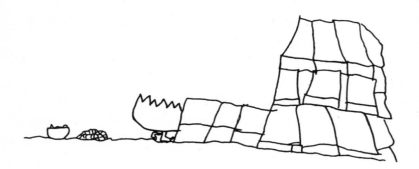

A hedgehog house, by Jasper. A happy hedgehog returns to his
new house after a feast.

5. Push straw, hay or dry leaves into the upturned box through the
small opening, filling it.

6. It's important not to feed hedgehogs too much all the time. It's
so tempting to want to feed them in your garden every night, but
that can actually be really harmful. There's no better meal for
a hedgehog than their natural diet, and if they become totally
reliant on you to provide them with food then they'll lose their
ability to find food for themselves. A small pile of cat food a
couple of times a week, perhaps increasing the amount in the
lead-up to winter hibernation, would be the safest bet.

7. Don't forget that hedgehogs eat all the pests that eat your
plants in the garden – they aren't called the gardeners' friend
for nothing!

Building this hedgehog house was easy, it didn't take that long, but
Jasper still talks about it now. It wasn't how good the house was, or
that the hedgehogs actually moved into it (although that certainly
helped) that mattered, it was the fact that we'd completed this
project together and it was a resounding success. Some of his ideas
had been used, he'd physically worked on it alongside me. Immensely

satisfying, I'd recommend this little project to anyone; you never know who will move in!

Challenge

If you have an area of garden or a piece of land that you have access to and permission to use, then build a simple hedgehog house and hide it somewhere suitable. Even if you don't know if there are any hedgehogs there, the natural world can surprise us – and you're giving them more of a chance than they had before.

It was in our first house together, a tiny two-bedroomed terraced cottage right in the centre of Henley-on-Thames, that Emily and I first came across hedgehogs. There were six houses on the terrace, each with a small, thin garden separated by wooden fences, and a busy central main road fronted the house, with car parks, offices and roads at the back and sides. We were surrounded by people, and it was the last place I'd have imagined to be the stomping ground for wildlife.

So it was with great surprise that I discovered we were regularly being visited at night by a number of hedgehogs. I'd come across hedgehogs before but didn't really know that much about them. Hedgehog numbers had declined drastically in the UK, so I was really excited to see these creatures in our garden right in the centre of town.

There's life everywhere – it's just that we usually don't see it. If you have a garden, then that's great and you might have hedgehogs passing through. If not, then think about looking in your local park, common or in disused ground. There will be life right there – and very possibly hedgehogs. Incredibly, London has hedgehogs in most of its city parks, and many people spend time ensuring that they are well looked after.

It was so much fun watching the hedgehogs each night. One after the other they'd move from one garden to the next across our terrace, squeezing through gaps in the fences, stopping every now and then to devour a juicy slug or snail. I soon became obsessed. I didn't know where they were living – under someone's decking or garden shed, I assume – but it made me realise how important it was for them to have somewhere safe to go and to enjoy the opportunity to wander freely on their nightly foraging missions. I made sure there were always gaps under our fence and into our neighbours' garden, unbeknown to our landlord! Hedgehogs can roam up to five miles a night in search of food, so free access within their territory is extremely important.

Eventually we had to move house. We'd outgrown our little terraced cottage and so with regret we left our nocturnal friends behind. Although we moved to a more rural location, we found ourselves right in the centre of a busy village, renting a larger house with a much bigger garden, which was simply a square patch of grass surrounded by a wooden fence. I wasn't hopeful about seeing any hedgehogs there, but, to my amazement, when putting the rubbish out one evening just a few days after moving in, I found one in our garden feasting on a snail. Needless to say I was delighted, and I vowed to do everything I could to encourage and help these amazing little creatures.

By this time Jasper was old enough to understand and appreciate what I was so enthusiastic about. We'd regularly sit there watching the pile of food we'd put out for the little hedgehogs. Cat food is the best option if you're considering feeding them, as it most closely mirrors the natural diet of a hedgehog. A good meat-based meal will maintain the health of the animals and give them a few extra calories to enhance their chances of winter survival.

As our new garden was so bare and spacious, with nowhere for the hedgehogs to hide, Jasper and I decided to give them a further helping hand by building them a house. This would give them somewhere to shelter in between their night-time wanderings, and potentially somewhere to hibernate through the winter.

The first evening after building our hedgehog house we pushed a little dry cat food down the entrance tunnel just to encourage them to take a look. To our utter amazement, two hedgehogs came to visit and both slowly snuffled their way into the house through the tunnel. As Jasper and I sat there watching this happen, our jaws dropped and our excitement grew. The hedgehogs took their time devouring the food we'd left for them, then explored the new, interesting garden feature.

It only took a few days for us to discover that the hedgehogs had actually moved into the house permanently and were preparing to hibernate within its walls. I dug out an old night-vision camera that I'd been given for my birthday when I was much younger but had never really found much use for. This opportunity was perfect, so connecting it to the TV, each evening we'd sit there in our living room when the light faded too much for us to see outside and we'd watch the escapades of the hedgehogs in comfort. They'd be in and out of their palace all night. It was utterly satisfying.

My hedgehog, by Daisy.

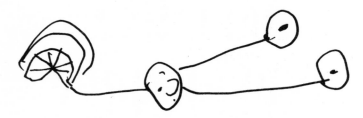

A snail, by Daisy.

Jasper and I learnt together that it doesn't take much to give a real helping hand to those creatures that need it the most. We'd given these hedgehogs a safe, secure, warm, dry environment to live in and were providing them with a moderate amount of food every now and then just to give them a boost. It was more luck than anything that they took to the simple home we made them with such speed, but if you don't try these things you'll never know if they work!

HALF-DAY EXPERIENCES

'Look deep into nature, and then you will understand everything better.'

Albert Einstein

Here are some ideas to get you going for a rather longer period of time – a whole morning or afternoon, for instance, on those days when you've had a lazy Saturday morning after a few Friday-night drinks, or when the kids are crawling the walls and need nothing more than a long spell out in the fresh air. Go out with a plan. The plan can change, but having one gets you out the door, makes something happen and gives you direction to start with.

Quick inspiration

+   Eat lunch in a tree
+   Carve a spoon
+   Make a clay pot
+   Eat a meal up a hill
+   Collect wild things

BUILD A DAM

Please do make sure that when you leave you remove any evidence of dam construction. Changing the flow of water can have dire consequences for people's land and local communities. Remove anything you put in the water; leave it as you've found it!

Nothing grabs the attention of children or adults more than building a dam. When it comes to moving water, it's a constant struggle against the force of this powerful element. In the right stream or river, you can see the effect of your dam as the water builds up behind and you watch it fill and flood the areas around. Sometimes the dam will burst, provoking a rush to repair and block the flow that's been caused. The beauty of dam building is that it's a challenge and an exciting game working out how best to stem the flow of water. It's such innocent fun – exciting, funny, engrossing and well worth the wet feet you'll all inevitably get!

What you need

+ Wellies
+ A change of clothes
+ A shallow stream, which might involve driving somewhere for the day
+ Rocks
+ Branches and logs
+ A spade
+ Mud

What to do

1. Once you find your ideal stream, it's simple.
2. Get in it and start building a dam. If there aren't any easily accessible rocks, then branches and logs can be used.
3. Start off with the biggest rocks, setting them in place at one edge of the stream.
4. Continue by building the dam across the stream, using bigger rocks followed by smaller ones. Build up the height of the dam and make sure all the gaps are filled with mud to stem the water's flow.

We were lucky as children to have access to streams and rivers in which to perfect our dam-making skills. In addition, my grandfather was constantly creating functional dams to protect his land from the erosive power of the river and to keep the water in his beloved ponds. It was a constant battle for him, blocking up leaks with cement and rocks to stem the flow of water. We were put to work carrying the necessary materials, hauling bags of rocks, even going underwater to feel where the leaks were coming from. Scared of sticking my hand into a hole only to feel a slimy, writhing eel, I'd pop up out of the water screaming, causing an outburst of laughter from everyone around.

Life was good when these jobs had to be done. Some days I'd vow to keep my trainers dry or water out of my wellies. The draw of the rivers and streams was strong, however, and there was little I could do to stay dry. I was attracted to the water – I always have been. Construction of a dam would start and before I knew it I'd be in. The first trickle of water would seep over the top of my boots, soaking into my socks, and within minutes I'd give up on the idea of a day of dry feet. It never seemed worth it – the best rocks always seemed to be in the deepest pools and I simply had to get them. It was so much fun building these dams, diverting water one way or another, creating 'swimming pools' behind the loose walls of rock and fast-flowing gullies to race little boats down. Whatever it is you decide to build a dam for, it's not in any way time wasted.

ROCKPOOLING

I don't think there's anyone in the world, from whatever background, who doesn't like rockpooling – or wouldn't like it if they tried it. It gives a chance to peer into a little watery microcosm in which life seems oblivious to what's going on in the rest of the world. Rockpooling engages the imagination on so many different levels. At its most profound there's an element of godliness to it – you're looking down through a sort of watery atmosphere and discovering unbelievably rich and beautiful forms of life on what seems like another planet altogether.

On another level, there's the simple fascination and wonder about what creatures and plants inhabit the sea – and who's eating who. Usually it's extremely difficult to find out, as there's no way to see all the creatures in vast open water, and when you do spot something it moves so quickly or instantly hides on your approach. Here in a rock pool the creatures are contained, unable to escape, and you have the life of the sea at your fingertips. So what *is* it that's down there?

What you need

+ A bucket and net
+ Goggles
+ Crocs/flipflops (the rocks can be sharp)
+ Wellingtons (winter)
+ Waterproof clothing (winter)

What to do

1. Check the tide tables for the area you're visiting. Aim ideally for low tide or a retreating tide because many of the creatures will have just recently been caught in the rock pools. If you're on a retreating tide you'll have more time to discover and search in the pools, and the pools will be freshly stocked with interesting creatures. On an incoming tide your time will be cut short as the sea will cover the pools, gradually forcing to you retreat back to land. Of course, this doesn't really matter if you're just there for a short time and you just want to look in a couple of pools.

2. Head down to a rocky part of the coastline (not usually where a beach is) and find some rock pools.

3. Watch to see what moves. If nothing does at first, use your net to stir the water. Gently poke its handle under any overhanging rocks around the edge of the pool to coax out creatures that may be hiding under there. Very carefully try to catch some of the rock-pool inhabitants and place them in your bucket for closer inspection.

4. Don't forget to put water in the bucket while you hold your catch.

5. It's really important to respect the life within these rock pools. Everything has its place in the ecosystem and any unnecessary disturbance can upset that balance. It's important for us

to encourage our kids to get hands on – to catch, hold and photograph the creatures they find. But please do put creatures back where you find them, and take care of them when catching and handling.

Challenge

Rockpooling is one of the best examples of how children are innately fascinated with the natural world and will actively engage with and immerse themselves in it, whether they possess a conscious interest in the outdoors or not. If rock pools fascinate them, then looking under a rock in the garden or climbing a tree in a park probably will too, if they're given the opportunity. These little hidden worlds are there to be discovered.

A day at the British seaside is what my childhood memories are all about – long summer days, building sandcastles, digging holes, paddling in the cold water and running out to get warm. My grandfather would always take a spade when we went to the Devon beaches close to his home on our summer visits. And I don't mean a small beach spade. I mean a real metal shovel. I didn't think too much of it when I was younger – it was just one of the things he did – but now I realise it was not normal, yet it's brilliant! The spade was used to dig the deepest holes, to make the highest sandcastles, to bury us up to our shoulders in the sand and to dig trenches for us to play in and jump over.

Papa was an inspirational guy in so many ways, not least because of the happy memories he left with his family. A Second World War veteran, on his 20th birthday in 1943 he landed at Salerno on the Amalfi coast during the Allied invasion of Italy. He'd joined the navy in 1941 as soon as he was 18, and was sent to work on corvettes out of Liverpool, escorting convoys across the Atlantic. He knew the importance of time and the value of making memories together. I have a handle on that, having spent long periods away from my family while competing, but it's nothing compared with the time he spent away during the war. It's something we won't ever understand as civilians – what life means after coming back from war. He showed me how to appreciate time and provide memories for those around us. It's certainly the driving force and sentiment behind this book.

TAKE A BREAK

Being outdoors can be tiring, especially if there are kids involved. You can't always be active and on the go. But taking a break doesn't mean that you have to be sedentary – it just involves changing the patterns and routines you usually live by.

What you need

+ Somewhere to stop with a marker point – a tree stump/ interesting tree/hill/riverbank/good view
+ Something to eat
+ Something to drink

What to do

1. If you're out for a long walk and the kids are getting tired and cross, don't press on relentlessly, just stop.
2. Climb a tree, sit on a branch and count how many animals, insects and birds you can see and hear from your new vantage point.
3. Jump in a trickling stream and build a quick dam.

4. Turn over rocks on the stream bed and take a look at what's hiding underneath.

5. If you only have an hour at home in the evening after work before the kids go to bed, then wrap up warm and walk down the street, watching the sun setting over the horizon or being directed by the stars.

6. Or go outside with no plan at all, then stop and sit until you want to move or until an activity finds you.

7. Sit on a tree stump with your child on your knee and see how quiet you can be for how long. Play I-spy as you eat a snack together sheltering under a tree from the rain.

8. Whatever it is you need to do to take a break, change the norm, move away from the 'easiest' thing and spend those few minutes with your child, make it happen. It's in those times that memories are made.

I look back at my childhood and marvel at what my parents did for my brother and me. Both mum and dad worked hard – they owned a garden centre in Gloucestershire and from 6.30 a.m. dad would be on the go. He'd rush off to work in his rusty old pickup truck, run around cleaning up, sweeping leaves and tidying up the centre before the customers arrived, then he'd spend the day in a whirlwind overseeing the running of the place. Lifting, carrying, moving, planting, delivering and everything else that came with the job.

As I got older I spent weekends working for him, which is when I learnt how physically hard his job was. I'd come home exhausted, although I never remember my dad being that way. He'd always return excited, pleased to see us, ready to play. Whatever the time, whatever the day, whatever the weather, he'd take us outside into the garden or around the village on our bikes. I vividly remember those after-school excursions across the fields to the river, looking for trees to climb, or when we dug the simple hole to Australia when I was very young. He really set the standard in my life, showing that even after a physically active day at work, making that effort was important and possible if it involved doing something different. Being with us was his break.

I found it really difficult to be like him some days while I was in full training, especially in the lead-up to a major competition or an important trial. All I wanted to do was come home and collapse on the sofa after a tough day of intense physical exercise on the water or in the gym. In my early years of rowing, that's what I'd in fact do – spend the afternoon and evening 'recovering' on the sofa, although I never really felt recovered afterwards. It was only once we started a family, where the jobs are never done, that I discovered that active recovery helped me much more than passive sofa time. Picking up Jasper and Daisy and taking them out once I got home kept my body moving, making my mind work and relieving the stresses and pressures of competitive sport.

Once I started doing this I very quickly began to see improvements in my performances and my mental well-being. They say a change is as good as a rest. Well, I certainly found this to be true. Having something to go out and do after work really helped me define the two sides of my life and appreciate the important aspects of both, and I became both a better athlete and parent for it. There's something deep inside us that gets a disproportionate amount of pleasure from making our children happy, even in the smallest of ways, so take a break from normality and disrupt the routine.

FULL-DAY ADVENTURES

'I only went out for a walk, and finally concluded to stay out till sundown, for going out, I found, was really going in.'

John Muir

I *love* weekends. There, I've said it. I feel privileged to have been given this opportunity to really appreciate them. Having never had them during my former life in pursuit of sporting accomplishment, I now value the time they give our family and treasure them like gold. Each weekend still feels like the first and they are all made for full-day adventures.

Quick inspiration

+ All-day expedition on foot
+ Bike ride with a woodland lunch
+ Fossil hunt on the beach
+ Volunteer for a wildlife trust
+ Spend 12 hours outside

BUILD AN ANCIENT BRIDGE

Have you ever wondered how our ancestors made their way across rivers in ancient times, or traversed boggy areas of the country into which, without some sort of road or bridge, they'd surely have sunk to the dirty, muddy depths? No? Well, here's an idea for a practical educational, fun, challenging activity that you can do with your children over the course of a day or a weekend. I'll warn you right now, though – it can turn into one big undertaking!

What you need

+   A hand saw/secateurs
+   A pair of gloves
+   10 to 20 long wooden poles, 1.5 metres long, with one end of each cut into a spike
+   As many long branches/sticks/poles as you can gather, all depending on how long you plan your bridge to be. Fewer means a shorter bridge, more a longer one!

What to do

1. Decide where you want the bridge to start. This is an activity that can be done in the back garden, across a stream, over a shallow pond or lake, or even over a shallow river. If there's water underneath the bridge it's a bonus, making it more of a challenge and much more fun. But you can certainly still have a fantastic time building this bridge over land.

2. If you're not bridge-building over water, then draw a real or imaginary line in the grass to indicate the edge of a fictional waterway. After you've drawn the line, the challenge is to not touch the 'water' on the other side of the line.
3. Take one of the 1.5-metre poles and push the pointed end deep into the river bed.
4. Repeat this with the next pole, around 30cm to the side of the first.
5. Pull the two poles towards each other from the top, so that they cross over at a point fairly close to the ground or surface of the water, creating a large 'X'.
6. This may take some time and adjustment, and will certainly involve significant effort, depending on how firm the ground or how rocky the river bed is. But once the two crossed poles are firmly in the ground, you'll be ready for the next step.
7. The idea here is that you start to use the bridge as you're making it. Lay some of the smaller branches/sticks/poles over the crossed poles and stand on them – they should support your weight.
8. It's then time to push another two poles into the ground a couple of feet away from the first two.
9. Once they're firmly embedded and crossed, lay more branches across the first two bridge supports. You'll now start to see how the bridge will form and progress.
10. The more crossed pillars that are set in the ground, the stronger the bridge becomes, and the longer the bridge is, the more stable it will be.
11. You can make some distance across your body of water or across your garden very quickly, and with imagination, discussion and hopefully a lot of laughs you'll be transported back in time to the earliest bridge builders.

12. The beauty and usefulness of a bridge like this is that its route doesn't have to be straight. It can be a winding, twisting bridge, around rocks, islands, trees, flower beds – whatever it is you need to avoid. Of course, the more it twists, the longer it will take and the more resources you'll need, but it's a fantastically fun way to spend a day in the outdoors with practical skills being learnt.

Challenge

These ancient bridges can be started and returned to time and time again. If you have the space and resources available, why not turn yours into a feature of the garden. It'll not only be a practical joint activity – it'll also improve the design and look of your garden!

Bridges are fantastic subjects for school projects too. Use online resources to discover the history behind them and help your child write a project on the bridge you build, looking into the lives of the people who would have built a similar bridge.

My brother, cousins and I built a bridge across our grandfather's small farm pond one summer when we were youngsters. My dad brought up the idea after reading about ancient bridge-building methods. Archaeologists had discovered the Sweet Track, a bridge built by farmers in around 3000 BC that was preserved in the Somerset Levels, not far from where we were at that time. There was a need to cross this extensive wetland area and so an ingenious bridge was built. The archaeological evidence showed that it was an incredibly well-planned construction, with prefabricated materials brought in from elsewhere and constructed skilfully on site.

Of course, we were sceptical of dad's idea, assuming it was a usual dad joke – 'A bridge of sticks, yeah, right, Dad!' Once we started work on the bridge, however, it immediately became apparent that he was correct, and what a memorable few days we had building it. The bridge wound its way across the water, finishing on a small island in the middle of the pond. It was stable, strong and sturdy. The more we built up the walking platform, the more stable it became. We still have photos of the whole family standing over the water on this brilliant little bridge.

For many years the bridge stood in the water, and each summer we'd return and fix any broken parts, adapt it and add sections to it. In addition, there were actually parts of the bridge that were alive. We'd used hazel and alder posts for the main supports, and when kept in moist conditions these species will take root and start to grow. In time the bridge naturally grew stronger and more secure – it had become a living bridge! I'm proud of what we did there and will never forget that construction and the knowledge gained by making the bridge.

Jacob's Bladder, by Trish Gregory (my mum). This was the first ancient bridge we built, in 1998, over my grandfather's lake.

MAKE A RAFT

Everyone should build a raft at some point in their lives. Over the course of human history, rafts have been used to cross the oceans, save lives, and transport people and goods. My imagination has always been sparked by the idea of drifting away on a rafting expedition, especially if the raft is one you've made yourself.

Rafts can be built from anything that floats. We've made rafts using plastic bottles, sealed plastic drums, wet wood, dry wood and polystyrene. With a bit of planning you can build a raft for hardly any cost other than time.

What you need

+ 2 wooden pallets
+ Plastic bottles/plastic milk containers/plastic barrels
+ A good supply of strong rope
+ A wood saw
+ A hammer
+ Nails
+ A long wooden pole/paddle

Jasper on a raft, by Jasper. A giant duck is in hot pursuit.

What you can use depends upon what you have at your disposal, easily and cheaply. You can start collecting these items in advance – there are no hard and fast rules here, but do try to make use of anything that floats. The challenge is to find a way to tie it all together and keep it in one place.

What to do

1. Start by transporting all your raft-building equipment to the water's edge. There's no point building a raft at home with no way of getting it to a body of water.
2. Lay the two pallets on top of each other and carefully cut out the top planks on one pallet with the saw. This can be tricky and will take a bit of time, but the idea here is that you're creating an easy ready-made frame inside of which the floating materials can be secured.
3. Lay the uncut pallet flat on the ground and place the newly adapted pallet on top of it. You should end up with a two-pallet-deep frame, with solid edges and a good-sized cavity in which to place the floating materials. Spend time fitting in the materials you have chosen to act as a float – if it's plastic barrels, two might fit side by side inside the pallet structure. If it's plastic bottles, lay as many as you possibly can side by side inside the frame, all with the tops securely fastened – you can use the wooden pallet offcuts to secure them inside the frame and keep them from escaping. If you're using plastic milk containers, these often have a handle, so ensure that all the handles are facing in the same direction and are accessible, as they'll be useful for tying the raft together.
4. This method of raft building really is trial and error, and is open to any method of construction. Using two pallets makes

the whole process a little easier, however, and provides much needed structure, the absence of which can be the downfall of any home-made raft.

5. Using the wooden offcuts from the adapted pallet, secure the plastic bottles inside the frame even further with the hammer and nails.

6. Once you've packed and secured as many of the floating devices as you can into the frame and tied them all together with the rope, it's time to flip the raft over and float it on the water.

7. The top pallet will form a stable, strong standing platform, on which two people can easily sit or stand.

8. Don't forget to take a long pole or piece of wood to use as a paddle. Rafts don't have the best manoeuvrability, so they'll need to be kept pointing in the right direction. On a flowing stretch of water they'll need to be kept well away from the bank.

9. Now head out over a lake or down a river on your own rafting adventure. It's unlikely you'll stay dry doing this activity, which is what makes it so much fun!

Jasper and Daddy on rafts, by Jasper. We are on our way to our island camp.

Challenge

Take a backpack with a picnic in a sealed plastic bag and find a place to stop. If you're on a lake with an island in it, you really must head over to the island and become marooned for the afternoon.

Why not build your raft during a day at the beach, using only materials you find there. You can combine building a raft with a great beach clean-up, making sure you take home or dispose of all the materials you've used afterwards. Always be aware of where you are headed, and check and adhere to local advice regarding currents at sea.

Rafting provides one of the best adventures a child can have, something that childhood dreams are made of.

FISHING BY HAND

Fishing is an activity that can seem incredibly daunting and complicated if you've never done it before. There are a number of factors involved, including the type of water you're fishing in, the time of year, the equipment you're using and the weather. But I'm not interested in the complexities of fishing. That's for later, for when you start to take it more seriously.

Fishing's not for everyone – you certainly do need patience – but don't let that put you off trying, as it can be incredibly simple, rewarding and fun. A young child doesn't need to know the art of the sport. Just keep it simple and find a way to catch a fish.

What you need

+   Wellies
+   A bucket/container/washing-up bowl

What to do

1. Find a clear, shallow stream.
2. Walk up the stream very slowly, against the direction of flow.
3. Carefully turn over any rocks that you come across on the way, looking down to the river bed. It's a tricky thing to do with the disturbance and ripples on the surface, but once you get the hang of it you can find ways to shelter the water so it's clear and allows you to see the bottom. If you're lucky, under some of the rocks you'll see small bullhead fish hiding.
4. These amazing fish vary considerably in size. The biggest I've come across was around 15cm from head to tail, but most are much smaller. They're incredibly well camouflaged and sometimes it's only possible to spot them when they move. Quite often they'll remain in position, even if you lift up the rock they're hiding under.
5. With one hand on either side of them, scoop them up into your palm or pick them up with one hand from above. It's obviously easier to use a net, but there's something hugely satisfying, about catching a fish with your bare hands. As soon as your child does it for the first time, they'll be hooked on bullhead fishing.
6. This type of fishing is fantastic as it couldn't be simpler. You're fully immersing yourselves in the environment, feeling the flow of the stream between your fingers, getting cold hands, and constantly thinking about where the fish might be and how to find them.

7. For children, having the chance to get in a stream and, let's face it, get wet feet, is unusual. If they do manage to grasp a fish and hold one in their hand it will be a moment that they won't forget in a hurry.

8. Once you've caught a fish, put it in the bucket or container filled with stream water and watch it for a while. Bullheads will change colour to camouflage themselves, so add some different-coloured pebbles to the bucket and see them assume another colour.

Challenge

We now take the whole day to go on little fish-hunting trips. We patrol a river bed in a team – me and the two older children – walking upstream and talking as we go. We stop when there's a stone that someone wants to look under, and usually we'll come together to help in the hunt. Once the fish has been caught, or lost, we'll move on, like minesweepers, slowly scanning the river bed. I've told the children from an early age that it's not OK to take the fish away or move them to different parts of the river. To me, it's just unnecessary to disturb these wild creatures any more than we have to as there's a knock-on effect to the whole ecosystem when something is removed or altered.

Draw, photograph and measure the fish you take. Build up your own record of your fishing trips together, if you're lucky enough to have easy access to the site you find. I always try to leave a stream in the same or better state than we found it. One way of doing this is by filling a bag with any litter you find. If everyone did so after a full day's adventure we'd all be living in a much nicer environment.

While I was growing up we'd often go fishing by hand. At first this would be in little streams, where we'd try for a while to keep our shoes dry by plunging our hands down into the water from the edge or while balancing on some rocks. We'd soon give up on this, however, as our toes would dip in and so we'd just wade right in. I vividly remember spending many happy hours crouching down in the cold fast-flowing water, peering into the shallows as I'd reach in and lift rocks to see what was underneath.

Some bullheads live under the same rock for the whole of their lives, and if we come and disturb them, changing their environment and taking away their homes, then they're at risk. It's easy to explain this to a young child because they can relate to home and what it might mean to lose it.

ROD FISHING

This is of course the type of fishing we all think of when we hear the word, but here I'm taking it right back to its most simple form. Anyone can do this type of fishing. Yes, it can take time, and sometimes you'll not be successful. But when you get it right it's a fun thing to do.

Make sure you always check for the type of license you need for fishing in your area. Children under 13 do not require a license in the UK, children aged 13–16 are required to carry a free license and anyone over the age 16 will need to purchase a license. Always seek permission from the landowner if fishing on private land.

What you need

+ Fishing line
+ A long, thin 1.8-metre stick
+ Fishing weights

+   Bait
+   A packet of fish hooks

What to do

1. Tie a piece of fishing line to the end of the thin stick.
2. Tie a hook to the other end of the line.
3. Put a few weights on the line a few inches up from the hook. (Fishing weights are tiny metal balls that easily attach to a fishing line.)
4. Uncover a rock or dig a hole to find a worm.
5. Here's the worst part — hook the worm on to the hook a number of times. It's a fiddly, difficult thing to do and not very pleasant.
6. Alternatively, tightly squash some pea-sized balls of bread and very carefully squeeze them on to the hook so that they remain in place.
7. Hold on to the rod, and throw the hook and bait into the water. Now you're fishing!
8. The type of fish you catch will depend on the type of bait you use. A worm will probably lure a different species of fish to a piece of bread. Experiment with different baits and see what the results are.

Jasper, Daisy and Daddy fishing, by Daisy. Of course the fish are avoiding everything we throw at them.

9. It's really important to be as quick as you can at getting the fish off the hook and back into the water. No doubt your child will panic in the excitement of the situation, but try to calm them down immediately, as panic will only make things worse. Take the fish firmly in one hand and push down on the hook with the other to remove it from the fish's lips. Hopefully it will be an easy evacuation of the hook, but sometimes it can be terribly difficult. It's just something that you must deal with as it occurs. Barbless hooks make the catching of fish a little more tricky, but the extraction of the hook is significantly easier. To me it's worth buying barbless hooks.

10. Take a photo of the proud fishing family together with the catch of the day, then place the fish carefully back into the water. Fish should be out of the water for as short a time as possible.

11. Fishing can be as complicated or as simple as you want to make it. This is rod fishing at its most simple and is exactly the way I spent my childhood holidays fishing in my grandfather's lake.

Challenge

I'm a strong believer in supporting the health and wellbeing of our rivers and waterways, having spent so much time on them. If you and your child are out fishing and you do manage to catch a fish, then return it to the water, allow it to go on its way and be satisfied with that. However, if you want to take it further why not bring a fish with you from your local fishmonger that you have bought beforehand. OK, you didn't catch it, but you can still process it, cook it over a fire and eat it by the waterside. That way you're maintaining the wildlife in the area you're in whilst enjoying a healthy outdoor feast and learning a skill.

During the long days of summer I'd often cut a long, straight pole from a nearby tree, untangle my fishing line, dig for worms and sit in as remote a spot as I could find around my grandfather's lake, waiting for a bite. On some days I was successful, on others I wasn't. That was all part of the excitement and experience. My grandfather taught me how to fish in this way, and I won't ever forget those days. When you see your son or daughter hauling up their rod as they pull a flapping, twisting fish up out of the water in utter delight, you'll feel so proud of them.

There are many different fishing methods, of course, and the more specialised your equipment, the greater the chances of catching a fish. It was, however, on holiday one year in Canada as a child that we discovered the value of using what you only have at hand to catch fish. We found ourselves one afternoon on a beautiful wild, rocky coastline on Vancouver Island. We could see there were fish down below us as we peered over the edge of the rocks into the foaming, frothing water. As keen 'rustic' fishermen, my brother and I were desperate to try to catch some of these fish to see what they were, but we didn't have any equipment with us. Dad just happened to have a roll of dental floss in his pocket, so we tied a limpet to the end of the floss (we didn't have a hook) and dangled both floss and limpet into the water.

Immediately we felt in the line that there was interest in our bait. During a lull in the water we could see the fish swarming around the limpet, which was firmly tied on to the end of the floss. After a short time I could feel a fish attached to the line, trying to pull it out to sea. I quickly pulled it up out of the water, and, lo and behold, I'd caught a fish! It was small but there was great excitement.

On closer inspection when trying to release the fish from the line, we discovered that when attempting to bite the limpet bait, the fish had got its sharp little teeth caught in the twisted and frayed floss line. Incredibly, the dental floss was catching fish in the way it was intended – by cleaning their teeth!

Once we realised this, we altered the way we tied on the limpet,
increasing the opportunity for the fish to get their teeth caught. We
spent a very happy afternoon catching fish after fish in this way.

WILD SWIMMING

This is something that people have always done – there's nothing new
here – but it's not an activity that's as common as it once was. Wild
swimming is a must for everyone at some point in their lives, and
although there's now a huge resurgence of interest in it, it's still seen
as something unusual. It's one thing to feel the water around you in
your local swimming pool – it's quite another to feel it outdoors in a
wild-swimming spot. This could be the sea, a river, a lake or a pond.

What about jumping into a deep mountain pool after a hot walk
up the hill to get to it, or gliding through the crystal-clear waters of a
hidden bay around a rocky outcrop. There's nothing better than this,
and few things more exciting for a child or adult. You don't have to be
a daring, brave and intrepid adventurer to jump into a muddy brown
river ... you might simply be wanting an experience to remember.
Wherever you are, whoever you are, seek out a suitable body of water
for you and your child to swim in – and jump right in!

What you need

+   Swimming trunks/swimming costume
+   Goggles (optional)
+   Wetsuit (optional)
+   Armbands (if necessary)

What to do

1. Find a river, pond, stream, lake or sea with a gentle flow or no flow at all.
2. Have a great swim!

Safety

+ Care must be taken when attempting wild swimming. You must always be aware of the risks involved in the water you're planning to swim in.
+ Check thoroughly that it's safe for you to walk into the water, particularly if it's muddy or not clear. In rivers, ponds and lakes, do not jump into the water without checking the depth beforehand. Dead branches, rocks, shopping trolleys, thick mud or simply the ground could be lurking under the surface and could cause serious injury.
+ At the seaside, be aware of tides. It's very easy to get stranded in the water and cut off from land as the tides change. Equally, if on land, and particularly in areas where cliffs face the sea, be aware that the tide might come in to such an extent that all the land is underwater and escape is impossible.
+ Currents and rip tides present a huge risk, so be aware of their location and avoid them. Never try to swim against a current.
+ Read signs carefully, and if in doubt ask or go somewhere else. There's nothing better than outdoor swimming, but there's nothing worse than having an accident.
+ Do not drink the water. Polluted or contaminated water can make you extremely sick.
+ I'd suggest you always take alcohol hand gel or spray to use immediately afterwards and then shower when you can

after your swim. It's not always necessary, but it's worth being cautious.

+ Unfortunately, there can be all the regulations in the world to try to make our waterways healthy, clean environments, but there are some factors we can't control.

Challenge

I'd suggest buying an underwater camera or an underwater camera case. Some of the very best shots are taken underwater, and it's great fun to capture expressions in the murky depths. My children love to film what's under the surface, and like me they're always looking for fish or interesting creatures. Swimming outdoors is a fantastic adventure and a memory-making experience, so capturing it is important.

How about tying your clothes up tightly in a waterproof bag and swimming across a river or, if you're lucky, out to an island. Get out of the water at the island, light a fire, climb a tree, explore and have a picnic. That's a perfect wild-swimming adventure!

I've grown up swimming. I was thrown in a pool at a very young age, and since that time I've never stopped. I went through swimming lessons, joined a number of clubs, took up competitive swimming – it all became very serious. I don't remember loving it – in fact I hated the competitive side of it – but I did it, it was simply what I did and who I was, and I became reasonably good at it.

The training taught me how to appreciate swimming, how to feel comfortable and confident in water, and, most of all, how to feel at peace underwater. Those moments when your body is full of oxygen and you're floating, supported, quiet, calm, relaxed, motionless – to me, that's absolute bliss.

The reasons for the decline in wild swimming are quite understandable. With the increase in numbers of swimming pools in our towns and cities, along with the historic rise in pollution in our waterways, it's always made absolute sense to me that we stopped wanting to jump into outdoor water. Rivers were filled with pesticides and sewage, as was the sea. Of course, this can still be the case to a degree, but government and local councils are much more aware of the ecological and environmental impacts from farming and waste removal, and rules and regulations are now in place. In the UK, certainly, our waterways are far cleaner and healthier than they were 20 years ago. There's a greater respect for our environment, which surely can only be a good thing.

That's one of the reasons I'm passionate about wild swimming. Kids love wild swimming – it's exhilarating and truly an adventure. If every river and waterway in the country were safe to swim in, then young people would be far happier and healthier than they are now.

I read about a wild-swimming spot a few years ago in a newspaper, in a list of the country's top 20 wild-swimming spots. As one of these spots just happened to be down the road from our house, one weekend we packed up a picnic and headed for the village through which this small river flowed. After dragging our huge picnic over a couple of fields we found the spot, and it was perfect in every way. We were in the middle of nowhere, a mile or more in every direction from the nearest road, which was just a tiny country lane, and the riverbank was covered in long grass, which led to the fast-flowing water of the river below. The river was only inches deep in the middle with a soft gravel bottom, and just a short way downstream lay deep pools for swimming.

It was the perfect place to spend the day with a child. We explored the overhanging willow branches, pretending we were Amazonian explorers, then we sat astride them with a makeshift fishing rod and tried to catch fish. We didn't catch anything that day, but we immersed ourselves in the natural world wholly and completely.

The cold water wasn't crystal clear, and I certainly wouldn't have drunk it, so we showered thoroughly when we made it home later that evening. Having started out uncertain about it all, Jasper quickly became confident in the flowing water. It was a safe environment in which to play, with shallows to paddle in as well as deeper areas for swimming. It was the perfect starting point for an outdoor-swimming experience. Now Jasper and I often go swimming in the Thames on an afternoon after school or for a whole day during the weekend. We have aspirations towards a long swimming adventure, but he needs to be a little older for that. Our dream is to swim for a couple of days along a river, dragging our camping equipment behind us in watertight bags. We plan to sleep in hammocks from overhanging trees at the water's edge and cook over a friction-made fire on the riverbank. It will be a true summer-holiday adventure close to home. I can't wait.

Our family wild swimming, by Daisy. There are those big belly buttons and long toes again.

OVERNIGHT EXPEDITIONS

'It is not so much for its beauty that the forest makes a claim upon men's hearts, as for that subtle something, that quality of air, that emanation from old trees, that so wonderfully changes and renews a weary spirit.'

Robert Louis Stevenson, *Essays of Travel*

For a young child an overnight expedition is the ultimate adventure. For many adults this is a big step out of normality too, and something that hasn't been done since childhood. We all loved camping when we were children, so why do most of us lose the will to do this over time? Just because you're not in the habit of sleeping outdoors and have become accustomed to the warm comfort of your own bed, it doesn't mean you should deny this true adventure to your children. Take these next few pages as a guide and make that brave move – go and sleep out in the wild for the night.

Quick inspiration

+ Make a mini documentary
+ Get lost
+ Have a wild feast
+ Make a swing
+ Dig a well

BUILD A DEN

I don't think the excitement of crawling into a home-made den ever leaves us. For this reason, I don't think there's a week that goes by when we don't make a den of some sort in our house. Look me in the eyes and tell me you don't like the thought of crawling into your own little space, hidden from the rest of the world, free from the problems and stresses of your life and your work, a place where everything troubling disappears for a moment and you're able to do just as you please. That's all a den is – that's what a den is to adults and what a den is to children. The only difference is that you're hiding from different things.

What you need

+ Somewhere to make a den – indoors/garden/park/field/hill/ woodland
+ Something to cover you – a blanket/ coat/tarpaulin/tent/branches
+ Something to eat and drink inside the den
+ A torch

What to do

1. If you're out for a walk, give yourself 15 minutes to make a den. It will change the whole day.

Jasper in his den, by Jasper.

2. Even if it's just a coat hung over a branch in a tiny hole in the hedge, a den is a den.
3. It's essential that no one in the den can be seen.
4. To kids, it doesn't matter how much effort has gone into building a den. If it's somewhere they can go to hide, it's special – together or alone.

At home we're lucky enough to live just a short walk from a footpath that runs up through some woodland. A few steps off the footpath, Jasper, Daisy and I built a rudimentary den one summer from sticks, logs, deadwood and leaves. We simply propped long poles up against a low-hanging branch, and the shelter started to take shape immediately. Hours later we had an enclosed dome over our heads. Completely covered in leaves, it was windproof and waterproof(ish), and inside we were hidden from the outside world.

I was exhausted once we'd completed it – let's be honest, as a parent you'll be doing most of the dragging and heavy lifting, but that's OK. We built a tiny campfire in the entrance and my cup of tea was that much more satisfying for my exhaustion – plus the gym wouldn't be necessary for a while. That den has been standing there for three years now and it's something we're proud of. The leaves might have rotted down, but every time we walk past we add just a little to it, keeping it going for a while longer. I think we're the only ones who use it. As long as we're here we'll keep it standing, and one day we all may even sleep in it.

The best den I ever made was inspired by an old bushcraft-survival book I was given for Christmas many years ago. I was desperate to try to build this shelter and when I finally had the chance I made a pretty good stab at it. It was during the years that I spent the school summer holidays in Devon at my grandparents' farm – we'd usually camp for a couple of weeks, but this year I was determined to live in my very own handmade shelter. Early one morning I started work cutting long, flexible hazel poles, then found a suitable woodland in which to erect the structure. I created a dome a couple of metres across by threading and weaving the hazel together, bending it right over from one side to the other. The ends of the rods were pushed into the ground to stabilise the shelter or tied to ends that were already embedded in the soil. Luckily there was no end to the raw materials I had available to me. By the time the living area was finished, the igloo-shaped dome in front of me could support my own body weight. I added a rough porch tunnel to the doorway, then covered the whole thing in layer upon layer of bracken and leaves. Hours later, this shelter was insulated, warm and watertight – my home for the following week.

I was so pleased with this little place. It was put to the test with the weather, and it mostly stayed dry and snug through a week of rain, tapping into that deep-rooted instinct in people to create safety and shelter.

I remember going back to school and proudly telling my mates about what I'd done. They probably took the mickey but the experience has stood with me and the skills remain. Sitting here and writing these words, I've an urge to build this exact den once again and sit in there listening to the muffled sound of the wind, the trees, the birds – and probably the rain – with the fire crackling in front of me, smoke rising and filtering its way through the branches above. This time it would have to be with Jasper, Daisy, Jesse and of course Emily, all laughing and chatting together. Life at its best.

THE SIMPLEST OF DENS

What you need

+ One pole, 2 metres long
+ Two poles, 90cm long
+ String or suitable material for tying
+ A big pile of twigs, sticks and leaves

What to do

1. Use the two 90cm poles to create an 'A' frame entrance. Dig the ends into the ground, if you can, and cross the tops. Tie them together at the top using a bit of string – wire, twine or even flexible tree root would work just as well.
2. Lie the long 2-metre pole across the 'A' frame so that one end rests in the crossed part and the other end lies on the ground.
3. Using wire, string, tree bark or tree root, a scarf, a belt or some other sort of flexible material, tie the three joined poles together to stabilise the structure. It doesn't need to be strong enough to climb on, just sufficiently durable and sturdy to rest other material on top.

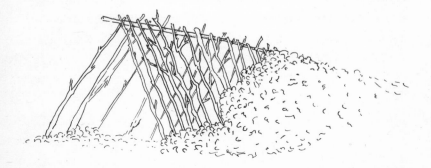

4. Lay as many sticks on to the long pole as possible to create a low tunnel-like den. It's as simple as that. Your child will love creating something with you – they'll be in and out, testing it as you build, getting muddy knees, no doubt. If you have time, cover it with bracken or fallen leaves to darken the inside and camouflage it from the world outside.

5. Remember it's really important to ensure you have permission to spend time and move stuff around on anyone's private land. If in doubt, it's best to move on and find somewhere publicly owned. These days there are so many places allowing den-making for young people. Most National Trust sites, for example, have woodland areas in which den-making is encouraged.

This is the simplest of den designs. Once you get into the swing of making dens and discover how easy and rewarding it is, you can branch out into more complex constrictions: teepee designs; low, camouflaged hide-outs; roomy family constructions; secure, long-lasting palaces. The world is your oyster and your imagination can run wild.

Sleeping in a den requires it to be safe and stable. This simple den is good enough to play in for the day, but the last thing you want in the middle of the night with young children involved is for a den to collapse when one of the children unwittingly rolls over into the side. For a den to spend the night in you need something a little more robust.

BUILD A SNOWLESS IGLOO

What you need

+ Saw/secateurs
+ 5 long, flexible poles of even length, 2.5 metres long or more
+ As many thin, flexible poles as you can find, length unimportant
+ A large supply of bracken/green foliage/dry leaves/moss – whatever's available

What to do

1. Find your camping site, ideally on soft ground with a flat surface. Think about where it is you're going to be lying and the direction in which you'll roll if you're on a slope.
2. Lay out the five long poles in a star shape, evenly spread, crossing at a midpoint.
3. Push one end of one pole into the ground. Once it's firmly embedded, gently bend the pole so the other end reaches the ground and you can push that in too. Take care not to make the angle of bend too tight, as this could cause the pole to snap.
4. Repeat the process with the remaining poles, aiming to cross them over somewhere in the middle.
5. This is a difficult process, takes a bit of time and doesn't always work perfectly. You're relying on the wood being very flexible and the ground being soft enough to push the poles into. The reality doesn't always match up with your plans!
6. A great tip is to sharpen the ends of the poles into a point, which will make pushing them into the ground much easier.

7. If the pole feels like it won't bend right over without snapping, it's no problem. Simply push another pole into the ground exactly opposite that one and bend them over towards each other. At the point where they cross over you can tie them together using some string. They'll support each other and still form a dome. As this is repeated with more poles, they'll all start to help each other remain in position, forming the igloo shape you require.

8. The 'dome' shape doesn't have to be perfect. We all have an image of the ideal igloo in our heads, but if it's wonky, off-centre or with a lower roof than first desired it's no problem. These shelters don't assume a perfect form and every one you make will be different – it gives them character, and something to remember and talk about!

9. Once you've got as strong a shell as you can make with the initial five poles, it's time to fill the gaps between the structural poles you've just set in the ground. The structure, with its initial strength, has already been formed, so this stage of the process is mainly to ensure that the gaps are starting to be filled in.

10. Using the same method as before, dig one end of a thin, flexible pole into the ground and bend it over so that if possible it reaches down to the ground on the other side. As with the five main poles, this might not always happen. That's fine – the main objective here is simply to fill in the gaps between the structural poles.

11. Keep checking what's going on inside your igloo while you're building it. You're aiming for a spacious, roomy area inside that's plenty big enough for you and your children. Sometimes it will need adjustment, sometimes a lot of manipulation to get it right, but remember it doesn't have to be perfect. As long as there's space, it's perfect enough.

12. Once all the gaps in the structure have largely been filled in, the space inside is adequate to fit everyone in comfortably, and the structure is firm and stable, you're well on your way.

13. Now it's time to be a bit more gung-ho with the construction process. Starting from the bottom, use any branch, twig or log you can find to fill in any gaps you can see. It shouldn't make a difference to the shape of the space inside – it's simply a case of filling in any draughty gaps and stopping leaves from falling through into the living space.

14. Finally, when you have exhausted your wood resources, or when there are no big gaps left in the structure, it's time for the really fun bit to begin.

15. Depending on the time of year, cut some greenery, branches, grass or bracken – whatever is easily available to you. Cover the structure with this, ideally from bottom to top, to further cover over any gaps you have left from the wooden structure. Layer up this foliage so it's thick and doesn't allow any light through into the space within. Give your child the job of continually checking where the gaps are. It's a brilliant excuse for them to get in, lie flat on their back and feel like they're really a part of the process and doing an important job.

16. One of the best times to make one of these shelters is in autumn. If you're building in woodland, particularly deciduous woodland, then the availability of covering for your den is fantastic! By this time of year bracken has turned brown – or is turning – so it's easily cut or pulled up, and can very quickly create an insulated covering. As well as this, or as an alternative, you can start to pile on the fallen leaves. Starting at the bottom, push leaves up against your wooden shelter. As a layer starts to develop, build it up. If there are sufficient leaves your shelter can be completely waterproof, warm and insulated, hidden and well

camouflaged from the outside world in no time. I absolutely love the look of a shelter built in this way. A huge pile of leaves with a tiny dark opening at one side that you crawl through to discover a cosy, self-built haven, hidden away from the world.

17. If you're feeling really creative and ambitious, you can try attaching a porch to the doorway. This can be added at any time, and it gives a brilliant extra dimension to your den. In the same way as before, create an arch from branches. This will require much thinner flexible poles; alternatively, use strong poles and simply press them into the ground and cross them over each other while keeping them straight. Doing this is simple and quick, but the slight risk is that if it's raining, having branches sticking out the top could cause water to run into the area underneath.

18. The longer the tunnel you create, the harder it is to get into the den – but often that's even more fun! Experiment as you go, the possibilities are endless. I've always wanted to create a curved porch, as it's a really great cold-weather entrance because wind or draughts can't then enter your sleeping area.

19. These tunnel entrances do, however, have the disadvantage of blocking the view and mean that you can't sit in your den staring into the fire long into the night. But if they're completely covered and insulated with foliage, these shelters are really warm. When you're snug and secure inside, wrapped up in blankets or a sleeping bag, you can really be outdoors whatever the weather.

Challenge

Building a snowless igloo is a resource-heavy method of constructing a shelter, and the process takes time and a great deal of effort. It's great fun and incredibly satisfying when it's completed, but if you don't have the time or the resources to spend on such a serious shelter, then an alternative is to create the shell with wooden poles and use a tarpaulin as a covering to make a classic 'bender' (dome tent). This takes far less time, and if the tarpaulin is free from holes you'll have a secure, waterproof shelter for the night.

SPEND A NIGHT IN A HAMMOCK

Everyone should try this! There's something about clambering into a hammock, perhaps that nervous feeling as you're deciding which part of your body to commit first. Your mind is telling you that there's no way on Earth this flimsy piece of material can hold your weight and that when you get in it'll immediately break. Then you go for it. You lean yourself into it slowly and gradually, listening intently to the telltale sounds of stretching and creaking, fully expecting it to come crashing down to earth. Your toes are the last thing to leave the ground, and then you're committed – there's nothing left you can do. You slump unceremoniously down into the material, lean back and without fail close your eyes and exhale in relief.

What you need

+ *A hammock* – Depending on where you are in the world, it's worth thinking about what type of hammock you should use to sleep in. There's no point sleeping in a string hammock when you're up past the Arctic Circle, though a string hammock might be just perfect slung between two palm trees in the Caribbean.

There are hundreds of different types of hammock out there now, in a range of prices, all easily found online.

+   *Rope* – Most hammocks come with the rope you require for setting everything up, but it's often worth getting some extra rope. If the hanging points are too far apart for the rope provided with the hammock, this extra rope might help you find a suitable location to hang your swinging bed. Ensure its breaking strain is easily strong enough to hold your own/your child's weight.

+   *Hanging points* – These should ideally be two strong, secure trees or posts the correct distance apart – 4 to 5 metres.

+   *Sleeping bag/blankets* – It's obviously really important to stay warm overnight, and your choice of covering will depend on the conditions you're sleeping out in. Sleeping bags that can unzip down the side are really good because you can use them as a simple blanket if you're getting too hot – if it's really cold you can snuggle right down inside and put the hood up. Please be really careful with children in sleeping bags and blankets. Ensure that they can't move themselves down too much and suffocate. It's a good idea to roll up or even tie up the excess material at their feet to stop this happening.

+   *Camping mat* – These cheap foam mats are pretty useful in a hammock, although you can also use a more expensive thin inflatable mat, if you wish. People often forget to insulate themselves from below and sleep really badly because they get cold. The trouble with a hammock is that your weight presses down and squashes your sleeping bag or blanket, so just as you would on the ground you need to create a layer of insulation underneath. This can be tricky to start with, but once you've managed to set it up correctly it's worth the effort.

What to do

1. Locate where you want to put your hammock up. This can be between two trees or posts in your garden, in the woods, by the side of a lake or in the hills. Wherever you find, you'll need the two points of support to be strong. Spread out the hammock in between the two trees evenly.

2. Tie one end to a tree or post support, ideally at around shoulder height, using a secure knot that holds really well but will not tighten so much that you can't get it undone when it's time to go home. There are a number of different knots that can be used for this job, but you might well find the bowline to be ideal.

3. Move to the other tree and do the same, tying the hammock at the same height.

4. Step back and check that the hammock is strung out straight between the two trees and as level as possible – the last thing you want is to be sloping one way or the other, so you should make any little adjustments that are required at this stage.

5. Spread your sleeping mat out evenly in the sleeping area of the hammock. This might be tricky, and it will probably require some fiddling with once you're in your sleeping bag, to ensure there are no folds beneath you.

6. Unless your child can get in by themselves – and it's fun watching them try to do so – help them to get in by lifting them. When getting in to sleep, I always find it best to get into the sleeping bag first while standing on the ground. You can then hold the edges of the hammock, open it behind you and gently fall back into it.

7. I've found that kids tend to sleep better than adults in a hammock. I think this is probably because of the smaller size of a child and the greater flexibility they have. As long

as they're warm, they'll absolutely love it and will never forget the experience.

Challenge

Spend a number of days in a row sleeping in a hammock during a school holiday. The more you get used to it, the more you'll learn the intricacies and tricks that give you a good night's sleep. It's slightly different for everyone, but there's nothing quite like swinging in the night-time breeze and drifting off to sleep with the stars above. Spending a number of consecutive nights out means that when you get back into your very own bed again, it will feel like heaven! In bad weather it's easy to string up a waterproof tarpaulin overhead by tying some rope directly above your hammock and draping the tarpaulin over it.

One of my most vivid childhood memories involves my grandfather and his hammock. We'd pitch tents or build our own shelters to sleep in, but he'd always sleep in his old canvas Naval hammock he'd kept from the war. He'd unpack it and spread it out on the ground between two horse chestnut trees that were growing at precisely the distance apart he needed. He'd then carefully untangle the ropes, tie one end to one of the trees using one of the knots in his huge knot repertoire. He was an expert at knots and always knew the best one for the job. I always tried to remember which ones he used and when, but, frustratingly, I'd always forget them. I now employ a mixture of all the knots he taught me put together – the same one for every job!

Once the hammock was roughly strung between the trees he'd move back to the first end, adjusting the height and tension until it was set just how he liked. Moving to the middle of the hammock, he'd turn his back on it, hold out the edges and sink his backside into the dusty canvas material. There he'd sit grinning, his feet hanging over the edge of the hammock, and let out a long sigh after all the hard work he'd put in, then he'd chuckle to himself as he watched us mess about by the water's edge or dad stoke up the fire, preparing the camp for the night.

Looking back on it now, I find it interesting what I remember, because I don't recall ever stopping and paying him too much attention – I was always too busy making a dam or building a den. But the image of him doing this is so clear in my mind's eye that I must have noticed it at the time. It makes me realise what children see – what they observe without obviously observing – and what effect adults can have on them; how we can shape our children's futures. Be aware of your actions. Parenting is probably one of the most difficult things anyone can do in life. No one will ever feel they get it perfectly right, but it's crucial to be aware of what you're passing on to your youngsters. It's a huge challenge to lead by the example you want to see in them, but it's never too late to change the way you behave.

SPEND A NIGHT IN A BIVI BAG

A bivi bag is very simply a big waterproof sack you use to sleep in. Stuff your sleeping bag inside, clamber in, and suddenly you're warm and dry, wherever you are, and able to spend a relatively comfortable night outdoors. Each of these points depends on a number of different factors that I'll try to cover. However you do it, sleeping out in a bivi bag is a truly fun way to spend a night, and one that I can't recommend enough.

What you need

+ A bivi bag
+ A sleeping bag
+ A camping mat

What to do

1. Find a suitable location outside to sleep, ideally somewhere with a good view.
2. Lie your camping mat down on the ground, removing anything sharp or potentially uncomfortable from your chosen spot.
3. Prepare yourself for the night by keeping on the clothes you want to wear.
4. Climb inside your sleeping bag.
5. Pull the bivi bag up around your sleeping bag, ensuring it's completely covered.
6. Lie down and relax. You're ready for the night.
7. Never allow your child to pull a bivi bag up over their heads. The nature of the fabrics used means they are waterproof, which also means they don't let much air through. Embrace the fresh air on your face!

BIVI BAGS

These range in price from hundreds of pounds down to just a couple of pounds and the quality of the bags in turn varies hugely. At their most expensive, bivi bags are made from waterproof, breathable material such as Gore-Tex, so any moisture you give off as sweat during sleep will escape through the material, meaning that you'll remain dry in your sleeping bag. This type of material will, of course, also keep you dry from any outside moisture getting in!

At the other end of the price scale are emergency bivi bags. These often come in a bright orange colour and are essentially huge body-sized plastic bags. They certainly keep the rain and moisture out, but the downside is that they do not in any way allow moisture to escape from the inside. After a night out in one of these – and I've had many – you'll most likely wake up completely wet through. At most, I'd recommend them for extremely occasional use.

SLEEPING BAGS

These are pretty essential when deciding to spend the night outdoors. I'm all for roughing it. I love to test myself, set a challenge and go for it. I actually enjoy discomfort for a while when I've decided to put myself through it, but I don't want my kids to be uncomfortable just because I'm OK with it. Thinking back to my childhood we certainly roughed it, but mum and dad would always make sure I was fine with that and that I was making the decisions myself to be uncomfortable. I really don't want to put my children off these sorts of activities even before the've learnt to enjoy them, so while I can be uncomfortable, my priority is to make sure they are comfortable.

A major comfort factor while sleeping outdoors is temperature. Being cold can ruin a night as I've come to know all too well in my own experience. More than anything this boils down to having a good sleeping bag and staying dry. As with most things you get what you pay for with this type of equipment but there are a number of things you can do to ensure a good night sleep.

If you're in a cool climate, try to get the warmest sleeping bag you can afford. Down sleeping bags are much warmer, lighter and more compact than sleeping bags filled with synthetic material. But if there's any chance of the bag getting wet then go for a synthetic bag, as the insulating material does not clump up like down does when it gets wet, and it maintains its 'loft' and insulating properties. Personally, I'd always choose synthetic for myself and my children for rough outdoor overnight experiences. Ideally the bag should have a side zip, which will allow for ventilation if the weather is warm or if your campfire is doing its job properly.

Dress appropriately when sleeping out, which means wearing a warm hat and thermal underclothes if it's going to be cold. The ideal solution is to wear little and still be warm enough, but it's a balance that's difficult to achieve and will only come with experience of sleeping in different temperatures.

BEDDING

What you sleep on is almost as important as what you're sleeping in. A good sleeping mat or natural insulation is really important to the quality of sleep you and your child will get outdoors. Nowadays you can buy all sorts of lightweight inflatable mattresses. Again it's going to be down to what you're prepared to pay, but some sort of closed-cell sponge-type insulation, however cheap, is better than none. Even a couple of inches of pine or other tree foliage laid out on the floor of your shelter will raise you up off the cold ground and provide you with some insulation. This is pretty important and will improve the whole experience.

When we really don't have far to go, I'll insist that my kids sleep on one of the blow-up mattresses we have at home. If we're going further afield, I'll make sure I spend some time on their sleeping arrangements so that they're as warm and comfortable as they can be.

Challenge

Arrive for your bivouac – the word that 'bivi' comes from – while it's
still light. You'll have enough time to build a campfire that you've
lit yourselves through friction-fire-lighting methods (see page 130)
and you can start to cook a delicious Smokey Joe's Fry-up (see page
144) over the fire. As the sun sets over the horizon you'll be sitting
there with your child happily eating the delicious meal you've just
cooked together, and as it gets dark you might send your child off
to find some long, fresh pieces of wood to whittle into suitable
marshmallow-cooking sticks. While they're doing that, you'll be
starting to set up the sleeping arrangements around the campfire.

With everything prepared, you both clamber into your sleeping
bags and bivi bags, then cook marshmallows together over the fire,
which is now smouldering away happily and still giving off heat.
Perhaps after that you'll want to quickly boil a couple of cups of water
to make rosehip and hawthorn-leaf tea (see pages 111 and 113) for
slowly sipping on before bed, sending that warm liquid inside you
to keep you warm through the night. As the night draws in, you both
tuck down into your bivi bags, then lie back and look up at the stars
together.

For the next hour you watch the night sky (see pages 72–3),
pointing out the ISS as it moves overhead, the four visible moons
of Jupiter, and the constellations of Orion or Pisces, and challenge
each other as to which direction you're looking in (see page 78). You
both fall into silence as, exhausted from the day, your eyes start to
close, but as you drift off to sleep you listen out for the night-time
creatures that are all around you (see page 66). The hoot of a tawny
owl rings out in the woods behind and the bark of a fox is right over
there in the fields to the east. Eventually, sleep overcomes you
both and you spend the night warm, dry, snug but ever so slightly

uncomfortable, always conscious that you're sleeping out on a rock-hard hillside.

The sound of birdsong wakes you in the morning, turning to your side you see the cold cheeks of your son or daughter next to you, still sleeping soundly. Looking over the edge of your sleeping bag to the east, you see the first rays of the sun breaking the horizon, its golden light shining over you, warming you up as you gradually become aware of where you are and what you've been doing. Sitting up, still in your sleeping bag, you lean over and peer into the grey pile of ash that only a few dark hours ago was the roaring fire. Holding your hand over it, you feel a little radiant heat, so you take a stick and gently move the ash aside. There's still a glowing ember down there.

Quickly you grab some of the remaining dry grass you collected the previous day, along with some fine pine twigs, folding them up as you push them all down into the embers of the fire. Smoke starts to rise – slowly, very slowly – then gets thicker, faster and more steady. A gentle blow into the depths of the fire and up pops a flame, soon catching on the grass and setting the pine twigs alight. Within seconds you've reignited the life of your little camp. You gently place some of the remaining dry wood on the fire, and as you do this your child stirs beside you. Opening their eyes, they watch you stoking the fire, already feeling the warmth on their cold cheeks. As the fire becomes established you put on some water to boil. No breakfast this morning – but it just doesn't matter. You don't need it. You're both full, completely full from the experience you've shared after a night together in the outdoors.

PUSHING AWAY FROM LAND

'As for me, I am tormented with an everlasting itch for things remote. I love to sail forbidden seas, and land on barbarous coasts.'

Herman Melville, *Moby-Dick*

If there's one thing I know about in my life now it's pushing away from land. Whether it was in the swimming pool as a baby, throughout my teenage years or in a rowing boat well into adulthood, I've always been lucky enough to find separation from solid ground. What I've come to discover is that there's something of value in leaving that solid, sturdy platform of land we're so used to, that place where we're embedded and in which our happy, sad, troubled, busy, rewarding, fraught lives take place.

Life isn't always easy. Even when everything seems to be going perfectly to plan, there's often a nagging something that's worrying or troubling. It may not have happened yet and it may not even be certain to happen – but I, for one, certainly struggle with worry. What I've discovered is that when I do push away from land, my troubles, stresses and worries drift away from me just like the land does. I'll leave them behind, ready to pick up again once I come back, hopefully, with a new perspective.

Quick inspiration

+   Write a story
+   Paint a picture
+   Leave a message on a stone
+   Pick up a bag of litter

CLIMB A TREE

Climbing trees take us back to our childhood. We all say that we used to climb trees, but I think there's a generation that's currently missing out on an activity that was once normal. You only have to spend a short time among trees to realise that children have a natural affinity and ability to grab on and pull themselves up into the branches. The desire is still there in us adults, and the ability certainly remains – so what's stopping us from doing it? Well, I suppose it's just not normal. It's not really accepted for an adult to be up in the branches of a tree, unless they're tree surgeons or scientists studying the forest canopy. Imagine seeing an adult up a tree in the local park – what would you think? The great thing is that as parents we actually have an excuse to be up there, and this excuse can be used to encourage something our children should be doing.

Tree climbing gives you so much more than a little adventure in a living, growing, moving and breathing being. There's evidence to suggest that being in contact with a tree is good for your health. Have you ever stroked a dog or a cat and felt calmer, more relaxed? I think

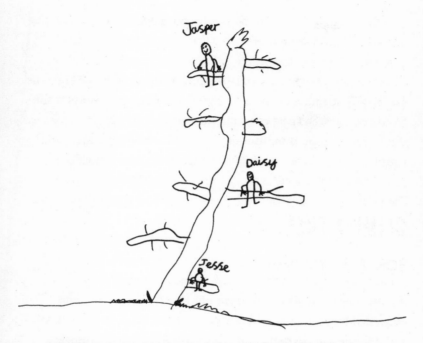

Jasper, Daisy and Jesse climbing a tree, by Jasper. The older
they get, the higher they climb.

it's the same when touching a living tree. So the next time you walk
past a tree just run your hands over its bark, feel the cool surface of
its trunk, breathe in the fresh air surrounding the tree and see how
you feel.

Climbing a tree teaches children lessons that perhaps they are
unable to be taught elsewhere. The decisions they make as they pull
up on a branch and step out on to another call for an assessment
of risk. Is the branch safe and stable? Will it hold their weight? Are
they going too high – or could they get higher? Will they be causing
damage to the tree by climbing up it, and do they possess the care
and consideration that's needed for the benefit of the tree when they
decide to climb into its branches?

There's also the need for absolute concentration when climbing a tree. It's well documented that in many young people's lives concentration levels, together with the ability to be patient, have declined. The obvious cause is the digital technology we all know, use and rely on so much. I can feel it myself – if I don't get instant results from a web search I get bored and frustrated, and switch to another website or do something else altogether. When I was younger and the internet had just made its first appearance, I remember that screeching dial-up tone as the connection was first being made, and then waiting minutes for a page or photo to load. It was all painfully slow, but it was fine because it was the norm.

Now, I just flip the lid up on my laptop and I've instant access to any information I need. That's what we have to accept now – the frantic time frame of our children's expectations and their ever diminishing powers of concentration. Tree climbing demands concentration for an extended period of time. It forces continued care and the sort of careful, precise movements that children just simply don't have to make elsewhere.

Climbing a tree takes you off the ground, away from land. As your feet leave the soil, you're transported into another world. You can be as creative as you want with this, telling a story as you go of escaping from the 'Green Figglegrimps' (a made-up name) that live in the grass below or saving yourselves from the quicksand that's started sucking you down into the 'Land of Safrinatus' (another made-up name) ... something along those lines, anyway. Tell a story, stimulate a child's imagination and sense of adventure. Climbing a tree is also a fantastic thing to help us step away from our daily lives, from the stresses, worries and problems that we all encounter – children often as much as adults.

I'm not suggesting you climb high in a tree – you can if you want to, of course – but I am suggesting that you have an adventure just a

Jasper and Daddy climbing a tree, by Jasper. One of our favourite places to hang out.

few feet off the ground. Find a spot on a branch to sit and talk, or just think. Share a few moments together with your child, talking about nothing in particular – or something specific. When you're taken out of your normal situation and given a place to relax that's so far away from normality – up a tree – people open up in different ways. Their perception of what they're capable of changes because they've just done something out of the ordinary to get there.

What you need

+ A suitable tree to climb
+ A backpack
+ Something warm to drink

What to do

1. Search out a suitable tree together. A tree that has a clear route up, with branches close to the ground, is ideal.

2. The beauty of trees is that no two are the same, so every new tree you climb is a challenge and an adventure. Some are much better than others for climbing. With some you need help getting up the first bit, with others the first bit is easy and then gets harder after that. It's down to luck whether you can find the perfect tree, but that's half the fun of it.

3. Encourage your child to get up among the branches. Depending on their age, sometimes they need a push, but once they're confident they're usually OK.

4. Always maintain three points of contact with the tree (two hands and a foot, or two feet and a hand). If a branch breaks – which can happen – you're still supported in two other places. Only move one limb at a time.

5. I always climb close behind my children when we're doing this, acting as a safety net. I've noticed their confidence and willingness to go higher and further in trees over the last few years. Now the oldest, Jasper, will go to places I won't go – so with him, job done, he's on his own! But with the younger two I'm always there in case of a slip.

6. After climbing around for a while, find a good spot to rest, somewhere comfortable, ideally with a number of branches

around to hold on to. Sometimes you can get really lucky and find a branch to sit on with a branch just above and behind it to lean back on.

7. Once you're all settled and calm in the branches – and remember this only needs to be a couple of feet off the ground in order to feel very different – it's time to have a drink!
8. Pour out some cups of hot chocolate and enjoy.
9. Enjoy the process of doing something so very normal in a very different environment. There's more to chat about, more to see. Talk, laugh, have fun. Enjoy each others' company. It's a chance to do nothing other than just sit, look, talk and drink hot chocolate.
10. Take a moment to soak up the sounds and listen. Listen to the birds, squirrels, cars below, people below – or simply the silence.
11. If you've brought binoculars, use them to look at the wildlife around you. Watch the tiny birds flitting around at their level for a change.
12. When you're sitting up there, it's amazing what you notice. Take a few minutes to investigate the insects that live above the ground: lines of ants walking a well-trodden route up the trunk, shield bugs that cling to the green leaves of the tree, woodlice, earwigs and the hundreds of other tiny little insects that live on the trees.

The varying species of tree are home to a whole range of insect species. Deciduous and coniferous trees play host to different insect species; trees with large flowers are rich with flying insects, such as bees in early summer. Take the time to look and spot them, talk about them, photograph, draw and remember them to identify later.

I remember a time when I was pursuing my sport intensely but was nearly broken, as much emotionally as physically. I'd been ill and injured throughout the season, and was unable to complete my training in the way I needed to get the results I truly wanted. I felt as though I'd let a great number of people down and I was struggling.

When everything in your life is devoted to a single goal, you do whatever you can to get there. If it's still not happening – indeed, if you're failing – it's very easy get caught in a downward spiral of nervous pressure and failure, and to slide into a dark depression. I hadn't performed well at a major championships, which meant that the funding I received to live off had fallen to its lowest level. I'd previously been lucky, retaining some of my funding because of my 'potential', but I hadn't managed to push forward and match that potential. My time in the sport was running out.

Emily was a trainee teacher at the time, and when we combined our wages our rent and our basic food requirements were just about covered, but absolutely nothing else. We both had to run a car, pay council tax and of course my expenditure on food – as an athlete who was expected to eat 6,000+ calories a day – was significant. I decided to work in addition to my training, which was unheard of among the people in the squad I was in. They all subscribed to the idea that if you trained all day, the remaining time in any 24-hour period was needed to recover from those exertions, so that you received the full training benefit and were ready to train and perform again the following day. Rowing had a seven-day-a-week schedule, so rest was essential.

*I needed to work, however, so I put an advert in my local paper which read: 'Gardener available. Afternoons only. Call 07*********' (the cost of the advert was per letters used, so I got straight to the point). For the next month I probably had a call a day asking for my services – the demand was incredible – and the fee I charged was sufficient to help us through. We still lived on our overdrafts, but at* least we were supplementing our basic wage. But all this came at a cost ... to my health.

I'd race out of training as quickly as I could in order to get to whichever garden I was working on in time. It would usually be around 4.30–5 p.m. before I started my second day's work, having not really eaten properly after my final training session of the day. Training was always tough for me back then – I was desperately trying to prove myself – and the competition every single day was intense. But one thing I excelled in was pushing myself. In fact, that's all I knew, so I'd drive myself into the ground on the water, in the gym, lifting weights or grinding out the mileage on the rowing machine. I'd eat the bare minimum to get through the day because I couldn't really afford the food, then I'd race off to do my gardening.

For the next couple of hours I'd do the weeding in people's flower beds, then any cutting, sweeping, mowing or blowing leaves that was required. Sometimes I'd enjoy it, but those times were rare. It was usually raining, and by the time I finished – in the winter, even by the time I started – it would be dark. It was a miserable existence and I lived in a state of perpetual exhaustion. I'd push my muddy tools back into my car, drive home, eat something with Emily, mud still ingrained in my fingernails, then crawl into bed completely spent. The alarm would go off at 6 a.m. and I'd do exactly the same again all day, although perhaps this time there'd be a trial or even a dreaded rowing-machine test, which I knew would cause me to vomit from the exertion and stop me from being able to do anything that required the slightest effort for days. But the gardens still had to be done ...

I picked up a number of rib injuries, partly because I wasn't allowing my body to recover. I remember very clearly one particular day while I was in rehab from a fairly severe rib injury. My season was seriously in doubt and it was looking like I wasn't going to make the Olympics. I'd just finished a physiotherapy session and was going to drop my car in to the garage to get an MOT, which it was probably wasn't going to pass, causing further problems – our training locations were spread all across Berkshire, and I needed a car to get to and from training and work. After I'd handed the car over I decided to go for a walk, take a break and breathe – just be alone. I was low, very low, stressed, worried and desperate; my health was poor, my immune system compromised and I was deeply tired, not just from lack of sleep but also from a profound sense of exhaustion. Years and years of stress and training were catching up on me. I was in trouble.

I remember turning off the busy main road and walking down a very quiet country lane. It was a warm summer's day, and as I walked I felt myself relax a little, conscious that I could appreciate my surroundings. I started to notice things around me: the hum of the bees on the ivy flowers in the hedge, the birds calling to one another and flitting from one branch to the next in their little roadside Eden, the white clouds scudding across the blue sky and the overarching trees.

I used to spend a lot of time in trees when I was growing up – they were always around to climb and I never needed a second invitation. The trees here were calling me, so I scrambled through the twisted hedge, grabbed the bark of a large oak tree and hauled myself up on to its lowest branch. I took a moment to consider my route, then pulled myself higher, leaving the solid ground well below. I surprised myself, to be honest. I hadn't expected to do something as strange as this today – not when I felt so serious, when I was feeling so stressed. The very goal of my whole life was under threat, so why was I acting like a kid?

Perhaps everything had become too serious and this was exactly the tonic I needed. I reached an even higher perch, then looked down at the road. The tree was easy to climb – a beautiful, strong old oak, with branches spaced just enough to enable me to gain height quickly. The road now started to look like a river flowing beneath me, and within a minute I was about 20 feet up. I sat down. My pulse had risen and my adrenalin was surging, but was it the exertion? No, I was conditioned to much more strenuous activity than this. It might have been the excitement of doing something different and a little bit unexpected. I realised I didn't want to be seen doing this – I mean, what would people think? I was doing no harm, there was nothing I could have been stealing or destroying, but, still, I didn't want people to think I was weird. Perhaps my adrenalin was raised because of that.

I sat there, hiding among the leaves, and listened. A couple of cars drove by, looking like speeding toys. Then a group of walkers strode past up the hill beneath me. I heard their muffled conversation, but they seemed preoccupied, with absolutely no idea I was up there watching in the branches above them. I remained still and silent until they passed.

When you're up in a tree everything is different, giving you an altered perception of the world and your surroundings. The pace of things dramatically changes, and your thoughts, now calm, wander in different directions. Animals treat you differently. If you're still enough, patient enough, you can enjoy some of the most incredible wildlife encounters while up a tree. What was most important for me here was that climbing this tree and sitting in it for an hour or so took me away – right away – from my problems. My worries about money, rowing, performance, my failing MOT, my injuries, my gardening and my illnesses all dissolved for a moment. None of them mattered while I was separated from the earth and my troubled world. It certainly didn't remove these problems or worries for good – but it did give me a break from them.

Returning to the ground, I walked back to the garage with a slightly different swing in my step. Of course my car had failed, but what the hell. I'd find a way.

FLOAT ON WATER

When we talk about pushing away from land, an image that might come to mind is of gliding smoothly across a calm expanse of water, accompanied only by the soft sound of the waves gently breaking on the sides of the boat. Although this seems so effortless, almost without the need for complicated equipment to achieve it, that's not always the case ... I hope to give some pointers here to help you depart from solid land easily and safely.

What you need

Summer

+ A boat/floating device
+ Swimwear
+ Towels
+ Lifejackets
+ Drinks
+ Snacks
+ Sunscreen

Winter

+ A boat/floating device
+ Waterproof clothing
+ Insulating clothing
+ A hat
+ A pair of waterproof gloves
+ Wellies
+ Lifejackets

+ Fire-making equipment (optional)
+ A flask with a hot drink
+ Snacks

What to do

1. Locate a suitable launch site for your water craft – here, we'll use an inflatable kayak. This might be a riverbank, a boat slipway, the side of a lake or the edge of a muddy, flooded field. It really doesn't matter where you go for the purpose of this activity. Ideally, it would be a long, meandering river or a beautiful crystal-clear lake, but remember that to a young child what's important is being there with you and doing something totally different that not everyone has the inclination to do. So whether it's that serene lake, that dreamy river or simply that muddy, flooded field, just find somewhere safe to take your first, decisive step away from land. It's perhaps most important to try to find a place from which it's easy to step into your boat ...
2. Start small, slow and manageable on a stretch of water that isn't fast-flowing, as it takes a while to build up your confidence.
3. Unpack and unroll the kayak, attach the pump and take it in turns to pump it up. Of course, it takes longer with your child helping, but it presents a challenge for them and it's important to keep them involved. Try pumping for a minute, then swap. Make sure they get the very last 30 seconds of pumping, so they feel like they're the one to complete this most important task.
4. Carefully push the kayak into the water, tying it to the side if necessary. The last thing you want to see is your craft floating off down the river without you in it!
5. Put everything you need into the kayak. The minimum you should take is paddles, snacks and drinks.

6. Put on any waterproof clothing and life jackets, untie your boat, if necessary, help your child in while holding on tight, then get in yourself. It's as simple as that.

7. Try to make a big deal out of pushing off from land together by both shouting out a grand countdown – 3, 2, 1, push! Then you're off, drifting away from 'safety' and normality. It's a beautiful feeling and an exciting moment, one that will be embedded in your child's heart.

8. It's now time to explore the water. Feel it underneath you, get used to moving the boat through the water and work together, propelling the boat along. Sense the speed you can generate and the control you can have over this little floating craft. Let your child move the boat on their own, then propel it through the water together. Moving a boat in unison is in my opinion the ultimate team activity. It's a beautiful thing when you're working together to get something moving, and the satisfaction is immense when you manage to get the boat to glide smoothly on top of the water. It's all about enjoying the experience, so there shouldn't be any pressure. You're simply trying to have a bit of fun!

9. While you're out exploring your chosen waterway, keep your eyes peeled. Stop regularly and take a look around. Scan the riverbank or the side of the lake, watch the birds and see what you can spot. One of the things I love to see is herons standing in the shallows like slender statues, watching the fish intently below them, their long, pointed beaks poised, waiting to strike. If you're quiet, patient and lucky, you might even see one catch a fish. I've only ever seen this a very few times, despite my years on the water. When it happens, though, you'll never forget it.

10. Luck certainly pays a big part in what you see out there, away from land. Sometimes there won't be anything to watch, at other

times you won't believe what's all around you. Without the luxury
of a whole week sitting there with a camera, don't expect to be
providing content for the next BBC natural-history programme –
but you never know!

Nowadays there's a whole load of different ways of getting away
from land via the water. The type of craft you choose will depend on
what you want to do, where you want to do it and for how long. When
I was a youngster we'd spend days at a time jumping in and out of
my grandfather's old blue and white fibreglass boat. It always had a
leak, and no matter how often he patched it up with his sticky yellow
fibreglass repair glue, water would inevitably find its way in. This
boat is still going, and is still used by me and my children when we get
the opportunity to visit, but those leaks are never going to be fixed.
It's the boat I took my very first rowing stroke in, long before I took
the sport up seriously.

Equipment

+ *Inflatable kayak* – For our family floating adventures we now
  use an inflatable kayak. Convenient, easy to pack up into
  the car, surprisingly quick to blow up with a pump and easily
  manoeuvrable on the water, it's stable and safe to use with a
  child on board. Once you've finished, fold up the oars, deflate the
  kayak and roll it up, and drive back home. It's fantastic for taking
  for a day out, and you can throw it into the back of a car just in
  case you come across an appealing stretch of water.
+ *Paddle board* – These have become very popular and are
  available in inflatable versions. They're fantastic for getting
  away from land and exploring a river or lake. There's more
  chance than in a boat of getting wet and going for a swim if
  you're a beginner, admittedly, so I'd suggest starting this activity

in the summer or wearing a wetsuit if you go out on one at any
other time of year.

+ *Lifejackets* – It's vital to wear a lifejacket when going on or near
water with kids, even if your child is a good swimmer, as the
shock of cold water can be devastating.

+ *Waterproof clothes* – Whatever the weather, waterproof clothes
are pretty useful when heading out on to the water for a long
period of time. Young kids do easily get cold, and getting
splashed is an inevitable part of the experience.

+ *A change of clothes* – Once back on land, clean, dry clothes are
always a necessity, especially for the little ones.

Challenge

I'm fascinated by what goes on underneath the water's surface. I've
always had the fantasy of draining whatever body of water I'm on just
to see what wildlife is lurking down there. Peer over the side of the
boat and look beneath the surface – if you're lucky enough to be on
clear water then you'll see things below. How many hours can you
spend watching fish flit around underneath a boat?

Cameras are now absolutely amazing things, and I really wish I'd
had a waterproof camera when I was younger.

Both of my eldest children now love taking their own films
when we go out on the water, and having the ability to take
underwater shots is an added bonus. When you eventually get
home, plug in the memory card and watch the footage you've taken,
it's often incredible what you see. I've taken hours of underwater
footage, and sometimes you strike lucky with a shot of a fish
coming right up to the lens or a crayfish scurrying along the river
or lake bed. It can make for a hilarious family session reviewing the
day's adventure.

A great thing to do is to securely tie on your GoPro or similar waterproof action camera to a long stick with duct tape or a bungee (you can easily pick a stick up from the riverbank). Head out on to the water and connect your camera up to your phone, then simply dip it into the water and watch your phone's screen to see what's under there! If you're lucky enough to be on a beautiful clear waterway, then the images will be fascinating. Sometimes fish come right up alongside your boat or on sunny days, if you're still, they'll shelter in the shade made by the hull of your boat, although you've got to be pretty patient for this to happen. If the stick is long enough, it can get right down on to the bed of the river or lake. Down there is where life really happens.

On Lake Varese in Italy, a location I'd often visit as part of the GB rowing team, there were freshwater crayfish in abundance. Every time I took my camera along and rested it on the lake bed I'd see these fascinating creatures creeping out from under rocks or clambering out of the holes they'd dug in the lake bed. At one stage I started to take bait with me to entice the creatures closer to my lens. I've got some great footage of battles going on over a bone and of a crayfish desperately trying to drag a chicken drumstick into a crack between two rocks. Giving yourself the opportunity to observe such goings-on is very cool, and to get to do it together with your child is fantastic.

Rowing was once an all-consuming activity for me. My body and mind were totally focused on the motions that were expected of me and my crew, and when we pushed off from the landing stage early in the morning, all the complexities of life would be put on hold. I'd be completely engrossed in what my teammates around me were doing and how I fitted into it – there was one job to do, the pressure was on to do it well and nothing else mattered. Life became utterly simple.

But you don't need to be working towards an Olympic gold medal in a boat of six-foot-six giants to enjoy that feeling. Your crew can be you and your child, with the sole goal of spending time somewhere different, away from land. Giving your child this opportunity is something they'll learn to appreciate. It's offering them a chance to step away from their own struggles, which you may not even know about. As much as we think we understand our children's lives, we don't really know their thoughts and worries. How many of us pick our children up from school and ask, 'How was your day?' only to get the single word 'Fine' back? 'What did you do?' 'Nothing' ... or 'I can't remember.'

It's like getting blood out of a stone sometimes, but that's just the way it is. I want to know everything – I want to know that my kids are happy, that they're being kind to their friends and helping those who need help. I want to know what they're learning, so we can talk about it at home. I want to know who their friends are and what games they like to play.

But I don't know many of these things. That's OK. I remember being like that myself with my parents. I'm not a big sharer of words with the people closest to me, as for some reason I think they already know everything. So perhaps my children follow me with that trait. But I'm finding the more I spend time outdoors with my kids, the more we talk – and one of the best activities for this is, without doubt, pushing away from land.

EAT A MEAL ON WATER

You've been exploring the water for a while, travelling along on the current, working together, with the paddles in the water propelling you along, exploring the riverbank and investigating the land from a completely different angle. This all takes its toll, and you can very quickly expend a great deal of energy without even realising it. When hunger strikes – as you well know – you have to catch it before it takes over the emotions of the young person you're sharing the kayak with. So it's now time to stop and eat.

What you need

+   Rope
+   A picnic – easy food that can be accessed and eaten simply with your hands
+   Antiseptic hand wipes/alcohol hand gel

What to do

1. It's always important to take a length of rope with you in the boat to tie one end to the boat and the other to some fixed point on land. It's useful for getting in and out, and for when you want to stop in one place, sit and eat.
2. Tie your boat to the bank. If there's nowhere to tie the boat, then just allow yourself to sit and float.
3. If you're on a river, be aware of other river users. Rivers have rules that are pretty important to stick to, especially if there's heavy traffic. On lakes, ponds and canals it's much

more simple, and you can often just sit and float with no worries.

4. In an ideal world you'd find an island. Islands are wonderful things, the source of inspiration and imagination.

5. Wash your hands thoroughly using antibacterial wipes/alcohol hand gel. You'll have touched the water, and it's not worth the risk of getting ill, especially as you'll be handling food.

6. Open up the picnic, sit back, chat, relax and enjoy eating outdoors away from land!

Challenge

Three meals in a day while on water. Now, there's a challenge!

AFTERWORD

I'm not an expert at anything, really. Perhaps rowing, but even that is a push. I discovered a way to make a boat go fast by training relentlessly, making myself the best I could be and harnessing the skills of my teammates in the boat around me. Everything I learnt was a development from the last mistake I made.

It seems to be similar with parenting. We didn't know what we were doing when Jasper arrived all those years ago. Three children later we still don't, but we've found a way to make our family work, to enjoy ourselves, and to raise some interested and happy children. As with most things in life, parenting involves a process of evolution. With passing years, some things will go well and some things won't and we'll have to change and adapt. Nothing is ever perfect, but as long as we try we'll eventually succeed.

To me, the outdoors is the important constant we need in our family to maintain a happy and healthy life. We make use of quality time we have together by doing simple, fun and unusual activities outside – wherever we are, whenever we can. I often don't know the right way to do things, but we figure something out. If it doesn't work it doesn't matter, when it does it's a bonus. Throughout my life I've built up some outdoor knowledge and skills – but like everything, the learning is never done and the more you practise, the better you get. Sometimes we have 30 minutes in a day to get out together, other times there's no restriction at all and we'll be outside all day and night. The point here is that the duration is not important; you can only do what you can do.

For us as adults we need to find a balance in life before life takes us by the collar and drags us backwards through the years. Before we know it, we've spent all our children's lives working, missing every stage of them growing up because we've been providing them with food on the table, a good education, a bigger house, a better car and everything else. Some of these are of course essential, but some of them ... perhaps not. Work and family don't have to be opposed to each other. It's simply a case of being as organised as we can be with our time.

My biggest fear when having children was that my performance and productivity would decrease. The exact opposite was in fact the case. The more children we had, the better I got at my job. I'm not suggesting everyone should go out and have more and more children, but I am suggesting that we should be aware our lives can be successful and happy however they develop. Allowing ourselves to separate work time from family time is important for our mental health as adults, as well as for our children's sense of worth and belonging.

Our children value time spent with the most important and influential people in their lives more than anything. When they are adults they won't remember the programme they watched on TV one Tuesday night after school, or the weekend mum was working and dad was sending emails on his computer. They will, however, remember the 30 minutes that was given to them out climbing a tree in the park or that time they got up early before school to watch the sun rise on the horizon in a field down the road.

The sun will rise and set every day of our lives – it's always there for us to use. There will always be trees to climb, insects to spot, animals to seek out and hills to sit upon. The stars will for ever exist, the rivers will always flow, full of fish to catch, covered by clouds to spot and birds to marvel at. Hedges will remain to shelter under, whether the rain is falling or the sun is shining.

A couple of days or just a few minutes is all it takes to change the path of a young person's life. How often do we break up our time, step out the front door and give our children one of the few gifts they'll remember, a special memory made so simply with the people they love?

I hope this book gives some inspiration to those who want it, need it, are looking, aren't looking – or those who don't even know what they want.

INDEX OF ACTIVITIES

CAN BE DONE AT NIGHT

SIMPLE, NO PREPARATION NEEDED

FOR THE MORE ADVENTUROUS

ACKNOWLEDGEMENTS

One of the biggest lessons I've learnt in life is that very little is done alone. If you want to achieve something you need others around you. This is one of the insights rowing has given me – the team is everything.

In light of this, there are many people in my team, and I'm thankful to each and every one for all they've done. This book would not have seen the light of day without Jo Bell, who believed in the concept right from the beginning, and Katya Shipster, who took a risk and committed to the project wholeheartedly. Thanks to these two wonderful women the whole process has been a pleasure.

To the team at HarperCollins, whose enthusiasm has shone through and given me the confidence to write these words: Georgina Atsiaris, Mark Bolland, Simeon Greenaway, Anna Derkacz, Tom Dunstan, Jay Cochrane, Polly Osborne, Julie MacBrayne and Alan Cracknell. And also to Eiko Ojala who brought this book to life through his cover artwork – I thank you.

Thanks, too, to the teammates who pulled me along for 17 years for millions of miles on lakes and rivers all over the world. It's being with these guys that I miss the most, now I'm not in the sport. There wasn't a day that went by when I didn't wonder why I was putting myself through all that pain and discomfort. All it took was a glance at one of those men for me to know and take another stroke.

I'd like to thank the coaches who guided me through the minefield of a lifetime of training, selection and competition. Keith Rafter and Dave Perry, my first coaches at Evesham Rowing Club, volunteers who showed me what true passion and enthusiasm for something was; Mark Earnshaw, whose efforts and commitment to me won't ever be truly known but will never be forgotten, who took me from a junior rower into the senior Olympic team; Jürgen Gröbler, who believed in me against all odds and allowed – even encouraged – me to live my life while we won two Olympic gold medals together.

We couldn't survive now without the support of our parents – perhaps we never grow up. Mandy, who was there at two of our children's births when I wasn't. She will always make the difficult journey at the drop of a hat to support us when we need it. Paul, whose advice is constantly called on and who calms us down when things are getting too much. My mum and dad, Trish and Chris. I couldn't have asked for better parents. They have given me every opportunity and supported me tirelessly in everything I've done. Only now, as a parent, do I realise how hard they worked for me and my brother Ali as we were growing up. I try to be like you, but I fail regularly. You've given me something to aim for. We love you all, and our children have the very best grandparents.

I never knew how much influence both my grandfathers had on me until they were gone. They were two very different men who taught me such a great deal. I want to be like both Peter Gregory and Arnold Shepherd. Although I don't see my grandmothers enough, I love them both very much and thank them for giving me the memories I hold dear and remember every day. Jasper, Daisy and Jesse all have the most amazing great-grandmothers. They don't know how lucky they are, but they will in time.

Emily, Jasper, Daisy and Jesse – my family. Thank you for supporting me in all I do. I hope to be a good partner and father to you all. I love the time we spend together, indoors and out. Let's continue to follow our dreams and make more very special memories together for ever.